CATS
and
CATHEDRALS

by

Patrick Boniface

First published in 2006 by

Periscope Publishing Ltd

33 Barwis Terrace

Penzance

Cornwall TR18 2AW

A CIP record for this book is available from the British Library

ISBN No 1-904-381-35-9

Printed by Antony Rowe
Eastbourne

Table of Contents

Illustrations

DESIGN

These eight Royal Navy and three Indian frigates are very significant postwar warships. They were the first postwar designs to be designed and built, initially, for the Royal Navy, although the Indian's joined the programme at a later stage. The Type 61 (Salisbury) and the Type 41 frigates (Leopard's) bridged the gap between war built surface warships and modern vessels built principally to cope with the demands of anti submarine warfare against Soviet fast submarines. The work on the design, however, started towards the end of 1944, when information about the latest German U-boat designs came to light. The technology and capabilities of these boats surprised and worried the Royal Navy; each would have been able to outpace and out fight the latest in service frigate types. The Royal Navy was justifiably concerned about this and the spy network had information that details of the German submarines had already fallen into Russian hands.

A high level meeting at the Admiralty in 1944 led to the creation of a study document entitled, the '1945 Frigate Concept'. A great deal of the discussions before the document was issued was centred on the success of the Loch and Bay class frigates. These warships shared a common hull and then specialised in either anti aircraft or anti submarine roles. Such was the high regard with which these simple and relatively cheap warships had been produced that a similar scheme for the postwar era seemed to be inevitable. Under the 1945 Frigate Concept', three distinct types were to be constructed and to save time and money, each would utilise a common hull and identical steam turbine machinery. The three types would specialise in a particular area of maritime warfare, anti aircraft, aircraft direction and anti submarine warfare. The first of these became the Type 41 Leopard class frigates, the second, the *Salisbury* and the third was the stillborn Type 11 frigate. (This was later developed into the Whitby/Rothesay/Leander class frigates as Type 12). A number of basic requirements were soon formulated including a minimum speed of 23 knots, in order to cope with the then latest submerged submarine speeds. This was later increased for the Type 12 frigate as underwater speeds rapidly increased. In the post atomic bomb era, general planners organised for a worst case scenario and accordingly it was felt prudent in some quarters to have the ships built in

5

blocks. The logic of this decision was that Britain could have been targeted by an atomic bomb and much of the industrial infrastructure of the country could have been in tatters. Prefabricated sections built at areas least affected would then be transported to a shipyard for final assembly.

Steam machinery then and now was costly and time consuming to produce and following a study in 1947, the decision was taken to recast the Type 41 and Type 61 frigates with diesel engines. Again, a great deal of information on the suitability and serviceability of maritime diesel engines had been obtained from German documents taken in the closing stages of the Second World War. The German Navy had been reliant upon diesels for a large part of the war and they had powered many of her major warships, together with the whole of the U-Boat fleet.

Salisbury was the first of the program to be laid down on 23 January 1951 at Devonport Dockyard. This occasion was significant for a number of reasons, but mostly because she was the very first postwar frigate. Her design had been put together over the previous ten years with lessons learnt from World War Two and the Korean conflict and took into account all the implications of fighting a nuclear war. The Type 61 frigate design was also significant in another way because *Salisbury* and her sister's was a brand new unique concept, that of aircraft direction. In the closing stages of the war in the Far East, some vessels, mostly American landing ships were equipped with a large array of radar's and communications equipment to contact and control fighters and bombers operating from Task Force aircraft carriers. These vessels co-ordinated strikes to ensure the best use of limited resources and also to protect the main force from enemy retaliation. These ships proved to be a great success. The only problem for naval planners, however, was that the scale and size of the early equipment meant that many ships were needed to perform the task. Whilst the most logical proposal was to put all the necessary material into an aircraft carrier, this would have impeded on the 'carriers main role.

It was with this in mind that designers started to work out the basic requirements to meet the operational demands. A frigate with a dedicated role could be built and after many changes of design, could also be sufficiently well armed to act as an escort for an aircraft carrier group.

For many sailors the ships had a very radical appearance when they were first shown in artist's designs. The most distinctively feature of the all-welded hull was a raised forecastle deck to improve seaworthiness. They were also quite a bit larger than previous frigate designs. Twelve Admiralty Range Standard Mk 1 diesel engines were squeezed into the hull to provide motive power and arranged in three separate engine rooms. Four engines were connected to each of two shafts by means of fluid drive clutches and reduction gearboxes. The remaining four Admiralty Standard Range Mk1 diesels were used for the production of electrical power, each engine driving a 360Kw alternator. They were not, however, connected to the two shafts. In *Llandaff*, a 500Kw gas turbine-powered alternator replaced one of the diesels. The large number of diesels was deemed necessary for a number of reasons, including survivability in battle conditions and because diesels produce optimum efficiency within a narrow revs per minute band. In another effort to improve endurance and economy of operation, the last of the class *Lincoln* was fitted with controllable pitch propellers.

The hull design had a double bottom where the fuel was stored. To ensure stability, as the fuel was used up it was replaced in the tanks by an ingenious method with seawater. The two never mixed and the stability of the ships was maintained at all times. Diesels also had one final added bonus over the steam plant first proposed for the frigates, very long endurance. All of these advantages, however, came at a price. The diesel units took up a very large part of the internal space within the hull, 29 percent of all useful space was taken in the Type 61 and Type 41 frigates. Later frigates, such as the Leander class used on average 18.5 percent for their engine compartments.

The Type 61 frigates main purpose was the control of air space around a carrier battle group or over an amphibious assault landing zone, and as such each of the class was equipped with the latest radar technology available to Britain. Each of the ships carried an array that previously had only been seen on battleships and aircraft carriers; large ships capable of accommodating the extra weight of the equipment. In order to be most effective these radar's were mounted high on masts. There were two masts that wrapped around the exhaust trunks that took the hot exhaust gases from the diesels away. As a diesel powered ship, there was no need for a conventional funnel and this gave the ships the somewhat odd appearance of having no funnel, except for the two exhaust trunks.

Of the two masts, the VHF/UHF communication aerials were on the foremast, together with a Type 268-navigation radar set and the DF equipment. A shorter mast was sited in front of the foremast and this was where the designers placed the ANU aerial of the Type 277Q combined air/surface warning radar. This set had a secondary height finding capability. Heading aft, the mainmast was of lattice construction, mainly used to keep top weight to a minimum, a four-dipole aerial, for the Type 960 long-range radar/air warning radar, was positioned there. The Type 293Q target designator was immediately below this and finally mounted atop a deckhouse aft was the distinctive 'hayrake' aerial for the Type 982 aircraft direction radar. To process all the information available from this vast array of equipment it was necessary to have a dedicated area to interpret it all. On all four ships a large operations room was provided between decks and all the raw data was then presented to the team of aircraft and fighter controllers.

Many people thought that the frigates could have been a liability as they were unable to defend themselves. These doubters were certainly surprised when the final design showed a full frigate armament. A twin Mk VI 4.5" gun was sited forward of the raised bow, whilst the then in vogue twin 40mm STAAG mounting was placed aft. *Salisbury* and her sister ships also had a limited anti-submarine capability with a Squid Anti-Submarine mortar on the quarterdeck. *Lincoln* was completed with a larger after deckhouse for a SeaCat missile system, which would have replaced the 40mm anti aircraft guns. However, the missile system was still in the final stages of development and had not been released to the Royal Navy when *Lincoln* commissioned. She went to sea with a single 40mm gun instead.

Lincoln and *Salisbury* would later in their careers receive major refits during which the SeaCat missile system would be installed on both ships replacing the 40mm gun. A similar refit program was never commenced on the other two ships of the class. *Chichester* by this time had been earmarked for the role of Hong Kong guardship and as such was stripped of almost all her armament and all her aircraft direction capabilities.

Llandaff, however, continued to operate much as designed, although the STAAG mounting was replaced during her career with something more robust and reliable.

The Type 41 frigates, meanwhile, shared the same design history but while the Type 61 was specialised to aircraft direction, the Type 41 was tasked with aircraft destruction. The *Leopard* and her four planned sisters were fitted with a main armament, which was the equivalent of a contemporary destroyer. Four 4.5″ guns in two Mk VI turrets one aft one forward were controlled by a Mk6M director with slaved Type 275 gunnery radar were used for surface and anti-aircraft operations. A Close Range Blind Fire Director (CRBFD) was sited in front of the aft turret, this was fitted with a Type 262 gunnery radar. The CRBFD could be used to control the aft turret whilst the Mk6M controlled the forward turret. Secondary guns onboard the Type 41 consisted of a twin 40mm STAAG mounting again with slaved Type 262 radar. *Leopard* and her sister ships were given a token anti submarine offensive capability with the placing of a Squid Anti-Submarine mortar on the quarterdeck. The detection and tracking of any enemy submarines that came within range of the frigate was undertaken by Type 170 and 174 sonar's, which were identical to the fit carried by the Type 61's.

Radar's fitted on the Type 41 frigates included a Type 960 long-range air warning and a Type 293Q target designation radar. HF/DF and a-navigation radar was also carried. All the ships of the class were fitted with stabilisers to ensure as stable an AA gunnery platform as possible., *Jaguar* was also slightly different from her sister ships in that like the Type 61 frigate *Lincoln*, she was equipped with controllable pitch propellers to improve fuel economy.

SALISBURY

Salisbury was the first of the eight Royal Navy ships to be ordered and became one of the most technologically advanced post war frigates to have been designed. The order for her construction was placed with HM Dockyard Devonport, as many in the Ministry thought it prudent to keep the frigate's construction 'in house'. She was laid down on 23 January 1952 with the ceremony being conducted by Lady Mansergh, wife of the former Commander in Chief Plymouth. The speed of her construction to launching stage was, frankly, astounding, 356 days after the first steel was laid on the construction slip, Lady Mansergh returned to Devonport Dockyard on 25 January 1953 to launch *Salisbury* into the waters of the River Tamar.

Perhaps the speed of the construction of her hull was due to the excellent workforce at Devonport, the next three years, however, would be spent adapting traditional working practices to the demanding nature of the latest technology, with which *Salisbury* was packed. Finally on 22 October 1956 *Salisbury* was commissioned at Devonport Dockyard, with the service having been conducted by the Bishop of Salisbury, Dr W L Anderson, DSC, a former Naval Chaplain.

Between November 1956 and March 1957 *Salisbury* carried out a full series of trials. On 14 June *Salisbury* visited the Pool of London and became integrated into the 5th Frigate Squadron of the Home Fleet. On 20 June she left London following a very successful visit to the Capital, this was followed by a day at Portland and then three days later a transit of the Kiel Canal for a visit to Karlskrona. On 1 July *Salisbury* left to take part in *Exercise Fairwind* that saw her operating with the *Ark Royal* before arriving at Portsmouth on 14 July.

Three days were spent at the holiday resort of St Ives in Cornwall for *Exercise Bullcan*, before leaving for a visit to the French port of Cherbourg with the aircraft carrier *Bulwark*. On 26 July the frigate arrived back at Devonport.

Later in the summer, *Salisbury* operated in the Clyde area before taking part in September's *Exercise Strike Back* until 1 October with *Bulwark* and *Ark Royal*. Another exercise took place for ten days from 11 October called *Exercise Pipe Down*, which concluded with a visit to Zeebrugge. After seven days alongside the frigate slipped and returned to Rosyth, where she secured on 29 October. November was also packed with exercises, with *Salisbury* taking part in both, *Exercise Sharp Squall II* and *Exercise Phoenix II*, before returning to Devonport on 26 November.

The next few months were spent in refit at Devonport. On 3 February 1958 Commander A G Watson assumed command of the frigate and the following day his ship was re-commissioned at a ceremony at Devonport Dockyard.

Eight days later *Salisbury* left Devonport and after a couple of days at Portland, worked up in and around Milford Haven in co-operation with HMS Harrier, the Air Direction School. HMS *Harrier* tested the ship's crew's ability to use their advanced technology and the giant radar set onboard the frigate. Having successfully passed the tests, *Salisbury* sailed south for Gibraltar and a period of time in the Mediterranean. In between exercises the frigate paid courtesy calls to Malta, Messina and Cyprus. After another later visit to Cyprus *Salisbury* left on 5 June for Malta, where she carried out a period of self-maintenance until 27 June.

Friday 18 July *Salisbury* was part of *'Operation Fortitude'*. This operation was in support of the troubles in Iraq where King Faisal and his son, General Nuri had been murdered. The aircraft carrier *Eagle* was ordered to the south of Cyprus to assist King Hussein of Jordan, as part of her escort *Salisbury* sailed too. By late evening the force was off the coast of Haifa.

23 July saw the end of *'Operation Fortitude'* and *Eagle* and her escorts sailed back to Cyprus. *Salisbury* went onto visit, Naples, Benghazi, Anzio. During the visit to Anzio in Italy members of the crew joined in a mass audience of the Pope at his summer residence at Castel Gandolfu, when the party gave a hearty cheer in answer to His Holiness's reference in English to their presence. Most of the crew also visited Rome, with some of them spending up to three days in the city. Meanwhile, Commander Watson, laid wreaths at the local war memorial and at a large military cemetery. The ship was also opened to the public and a party was organised onboard for children from a local orphanage. *Salisbury*

went onto visit Toulon, before leaving the Mediterranean on 21 November when she left Gibraltar for the return leg to Devonport. Some interesting statistics during *Salisbury's* time in the Mediterranean saw the crew drink no less than 2,790 pints of rum, 6,750 tins of milk, 669 tins of 'Bluebell', 300 tons of potatoes and also used 72 galvanised buckets. Later in the month of November she continued to operate as part of the 5th Frigate Squadron in British waters and this included a period in Icelandic waters protecting British trawler-men and their ships from Icelandic gunboats during what became known as the First Cod War. *Salisbury* stayed in British waters until June 1959.

The following month, the frigate crossed the North Atlantic to visit the United States and Canada. On 10 July she arrived at Norfolk, Virginia and was welcomed by the large number of American servicemen at America's largest navy base. *Salisbury* was there was to take part in *Exercise Riptide,* which started on 14 July and lasted for nine days. The next day *Salisbury* arrived at Bermuda and her arrival had been timed to coincide with the 350th anniversary of British rule on the island.

August was packed with port visits in Canada, by the end of the month, *Salisbury* had visited Halifax, St John's, Charleston, Montreal and Toronto. The following month it was the turn of the United States and the frigate sailed into Cleveland on 4 September before again calling on Canada with visits to Kingston, Ontario and St Johns in Newfoundland. Following this visit, *Salisbury* started her crossing of the Atlantic and arrived at Devonport on 21 September. Seven days later Commander J K Stevens assumed command. On 29 September 1959 *Salisbury* was officially re-commissioned at Devonport

Salisbury was at Portland with the other ships from the 5th Frigate Squadron, *Torquay, Tenby* and *Scarborough* from 6 October until mid November. She also visited Milford Haven to conduct the Aircraft Direction phase of her work-up. In November she took part in *Exercise Sharp Squall IV,* that kept the ship occupied until 27 November. The next day *Salisbury* sailed back into harbour at Devonport.

Christmas and New Year was spent at Devonport. 1960 started for *Salisbury* with a deployment to Icelandic waters at the beginning of February for anti submarine exercises with *Torquay, Palladin* and *Tenby.* Later in the month she sailed with 5th FS for Far East.

Salisbury was detached to act as plane-guard for *Albion* during *Flyex* in the Mediterranean. Whilst in the Mediterranean *Salisbury* was part of a large Royal Navy force that was present for a Royal Occasion. Several officers were presented to his Majesty King Paul of the Hellenes and the Crown Prince during a visit to Athens with the aircraft carrier *Albion*.

Salisbury left the Mediterranean at the end of April and transited the Suez Canal with the aircraft carrier, before arriving at Aden and onto Singapore. The summer months were spent exercising with local navies and *Salisbury* remained close to *Albion* throughout. There were port visits to Singapore and Manila as well.

At the end of July *Salisbury* sailed for Hong Kong to take over local guardship duties for a month. From Hong Kong *Salisbury* sailed north to join the Far East Fleet in exercises prior to visiting Kagoshima on the island of Kyushu and Tokyo. This was followed by exercises with the US 7th Fleet off the Philippines before returning to Singapore. After a few weeks there, *Salisbury* sailed for Trincomalee.

After spending nine days at Trincomalee, the frigate put to sea and operated with *Albion*. It was during a night-time exercise that tragedy was just averted. *Albion* and *Salisbury* had a close shave when a collision was narrowly avoided in the early hours of one exercise. The frigate pulled ahead of the aircraft carrier and came close to being crushed beneath *Albion's* bows. 7 August 1960 saw the appointment of Commander W Fitzgerald to the command of *Salisbury*.

Later in the deployment on 24 October *Salisbury* visited Karachi with the 5th FS where all four ships participated in a CENTO exercise. *Salisbury* and the other ships left port on 10 November and after seven days steaming arrived at the hot and dusty destination of Dar-es-salaam. Seven days were spent alongside and many visitors and dignitaries were welcomed onboard by the officers and men of the frigate. *Salisbury* left port on 24 November and the next day arrived at Mombassa for an overnight stay. The frigate's next destination was Aden, which was reached on 30 November.

Aden was a desolate and uninviting destination and the ship spent just a couple of days there before starting her return journey to the United Kingdom, via the Suez Canal. *Salisbury* stopped off at Gibraltar and arrived at Devonport on 15 December.

Christmas leave was granted to the crew, but upon their return in the New Year of 1961, *Salisbury's* first deployment was to act as a plane guard to an aircraft carrier before arriving off Londonderry at the end of January. The following month saw her taking part in *JSC 114* until 24 February. Greenock was visited at the beginning of March, where the frigate participated in *FOSM 'Bravo'* until 10 March. Two days later she arrived at Portland where she remained for the next nine days. On 22 March *Salisbury* arrived at the French coastal port of Boulonge for a five-day visit before arriving back at Portsmouth for Easter leave. *Salisbury* was back at sea on 17 April and took part in fishery protection patrols

A highlight of the commission occurred in April 1961 when *Salisbury* escorted *Britannia* with HM Queen Mother embarked from Portsmouth to Gibraltar. During the passage Commander J K Stevens was transferred by jackstay for lunch with her majesty. Later in the month, *Salisbury* was at Gibraltar and also paid a visit to the port of Oporto. The frigate returned home to British waters in May and before entering refit at Devonport paid a visit to the island of Ismay on 30 May. *Salisbury* arrived at Devonport on June 5 1961 and was soon taken in hand for a major reconstructive refit. For the next sixteen months *Salisbury* was in dockyard hands. When she completed her refit she was amongst the most modern warships afloat. *Salisbury's* Type 960 radar was removed and the original lattice mainmast replaced by a wider and taller plated mast. A massive AKE-2 double bedstead aerial, with a Type 1010 interrogator on top for the Type 965 long-range air warning radar was fitted. The Type 293Q target indicating radar aerial was moved to a brand new position on a platform near the top of the frigates' foremast. There it formed part of the ship's ESM array. A Mk5 twin 40mm gun replaced the STAAG mounting, with its director and slaved Type 262 radar. The director for this weapon sat upon a newly enlarged after superstructure. In addition to these changes the mast supporting the Type 282 radar aerial was enlarged. On 28 September 1962 the refit was completed and *Salisbury* commenced the long process of work-up that continued throughout the autumn and winter of 1962 and into the first few months of 1963. When she re-commissioned into service, she joined the 4th Frigate Squadron and operated initially in British waters.

Salisbury left Portsmouth to visit the German port of Luebeck, where she arrived on 16 January for a five-day visit, before assuming plane-guard duties. On 30 January she was at Harwich for an overnight stay whilst the next day *Salisbury* returned to Portsmouth. After taking part in small exercises in February, the frigate took part in the major exercise *Dawn Breeze 8*, which finished on 18 March. Two days later *Salisbury* took part in *JSC 123*. At the end of the exercises *Salisbury* was in the Clyde area to assist the submarine training programme S/M 3, where she remained until 22 April. Between 22 April and 27 April, *Salisbury* was consort to the brand new nuclear powered submarine *Dreadnought*. Security around this Britain's first nuclear submarine was tight and on a number of occasions *Salisbury* and the other escorts had to shoo away a number of vessels that got too close for comfort. Two days later the frigate arrived back at Portsmouth.

After leaving Portsmouth, *Salisbury* started her deployment to the Far East and paid brief visits to Gibraltar, Malta, Suez, Aden and Gan whilst en route to Singapore, which was reached on 2 July. *Salisbury* was docked for essential maintenance at the Dockyard until 23 July. The next day, the ship put to sea to take part, along with other Royal Navy units in five days of training and exercises under the banner of *FOTEX*. In July *Salisbury* took part in twelve-day exercise off Malaysia's East Coast with *Albion, Duchess, Otago, Quiberon, Cambrian, Vendetta* and *Plymouth*. At the end the exercise she refuelled at Gan before sailing back to Singapore.

After some days at sea in mid August with the aircraft carrier *Ark Royal Salisbury* was back in port on 17 August. Three days later she slipped again and made for the island of Gan. On 30 August *Salisbury* arrived at Aden and was attached to the aircraft carrier *Victorious*, with whom she remained until 13 October 1963 during the Indonesian crisis. Throughout this period the frigate was on a high state of alert. The terrorist threat was real and everyone onboard during these patrols watched for any sign of hostile activity. Ships and small boats were stopped and inspected to ensure arms did not reach rebel hands.

Next port of call for *Salisbury* was Hong Kong on 19 October. She remained in port for nine days, then slipped her moorings and visited the island of Cebu before operating with the aircraft carrier *Victorious* until 25 November. Four days were spent at Singapore assisting in the work-up of the Battle class destroyer *Barrosa* between 25-29 November. Upon her return to the dockyard *Salisbury* conducted self-maintenance until 7 December.

Salisbury escorted both *Victorious* and *Albion* before arriving on 20 December in the Tawau area. The patrols continued until 11 January 1964, when she returned to Singapore. She remained in port until 31 January when the frigate left Singapore *Salisbury* had onboard as passengers men from 45 Commando en route to East Africa to maintain law and order following a mutiny. The aircraft carrier *Albion* also had men from 45 Commando onboard and sailed with *Salisbury* to Zanzibar and on to Mombassa, where she arrived on 9 February.

The arrival of this force quelled the mutiny and peace was soon restored. By mid March 1964 *Salisbury* was at Kilindini harbour. Later in the month she had arrived at Aden and a fast transit through the Suez Canal. When she arrived at Malta, *Salisbury* entered dock on the island in order for the bottom of her hull to be scrapped.

Spring and summer 1964 saw *Salisbury* operating in home waters as part of 23rd Escort Squadron which included a month long series of anti submarine exercises off Londonderry.

On 25 June 1964 *Salisbury* and *Diamond* collided in shallow water off Spithead in the Tab Tower area while both ships were practising for Sea Days and members of the Staff Colleges were embarked as observers. While exchanging stations *Diamond* came too close to *Salisbury* and because of the shallow water effect, *Diamond's* stern was sucked into *Salisbury's* bow damaging it badly. *Salisbury* was holed in 2 deck forward and was declared un-seaworthy. Temporary repairs were made at Portsmouth before sailing to Devonport for permanent repairs, which were completed in July 1964.

Early in August 1964 *Salisbury* visited Worthing in Sussex. The ship anchored two miles off the Pier owing to no deep water and the local council arranged for a 'DUKW' and shore boats, together with four fine weather days, made for a very enjoyable time. Every man was given a card entitling him to free admission, to a very large number of the town's amenities.

A group of handicapped children from the local John Horniman School, were brought onboard for a traditional pirates party. Each of the children was officially enrolled as a member of a crew of pirates. In total nearly 500 people visited the ship on the afternoon of Saturday 15 August.

August also saw *Salisbury* at Portsmouth for the last annual review of the Home Fleet. Present were *London* (F/S Admiral Sir Charles Madden (CinC Home Fleet), *Lion* (F/S Flotilla's Home Fleet), *Aurora, Agincourt, Carysfort, Devonshire, Diamond, Dundas, Eskimo, Leander, Londonderry, Lowestoft, Murray, Pellew, Puma, Relentless, Rhyl, Galatea, Salisbury* and *Olna*.

After summer leave the ship left Portsmouth and went onto visit Amsterdam and Bordeaux in October. Before returning to port to enter into refit.

On 8 December 1964 Commander R D Johnson took command of the frigate. Work, however, continued on the frigate. The work was almost complete when on 11 May 1965, the commissioning cake was cut by Commander Johnson's wife and Mrs Ralph, the wife of the ship's coxswain.

Salisbury worked up off Portland in June and July before joining the 21st Escort Squadron of the Home Fleet. The following month, she sailed north to Scotland, where on 8 to 10 August 1965 she was on the Clyde for Royal Review. After this event *Salisbury* escorted *Britannia* (with HM the Queen and Duke of Edinburgh on the Queen's five-day summer cruise around Scotland). On completion of the cruise, *Salisbury* visited the Channel Islands before exercising off Cape Wrath.

In September 1965 five days were spent visiting Stockholm prior to re-deployment leave and maintenance at Devonport. This was completed by the early days of November 1965. After storing the ship for the passage to the Far East, *Salisbury* left Devonport on 17 November 1965 and was joined by the frigate *Dido* at Gibraltar.

The pair continued east and on 1 December arrived at Aden and was joined by another squadron member *Berwick*. Subsequently, *Salisbury* and *Dido* were sent to join the Beira Patrol and then to rendezvous with the carrier *Eagle*. However, before they could achieve this both frigates were ordered back to Aden where they exercised until 14 December. Later both sailed for Singapore, arriving three days after Christmas.

After a maintenance period, which lasted until 10 January 1966, *Salisbury* left Singapore on 15 January for patrol duties in connection with the Indonesian Confrontation and remained at sea until 5 March, including four weeks in the Tawau area of Sabah. Her job was to prevent Indonesian craft landing men and guns in Malaysia.

Between March and April 1966 *Salisbury* was operating in the Singapore area and Malacca Straits including a short assisted maintenance period at Singapore. After a four-week Confrontation patrol, *Salisbury* sailed for Hong Kong, arriving on 2 May 1966. Three days later on 5 May *Salisbury's* latest commanding officer, Commander H M Ellis took up his post during a maintenance period.

On 18 May *Salisbury* left Singapore and in the next two months spent periods of time operating with *Forth* and the aircraft carrier *Eagle* before arriving at Hong Kong on 7 June. On 11 June she left the colony to resume operations with *Eagle* as they sailed towards Singapore. The frigate would later in July visit the exotic city of Bangkok on 29 July for a four-day stay. After a hugely successful visit the warship returned to Singapore.

Allan 'Buster' Brown recalls "We left Singapore for the UK in the late summer of 1966 and stopped en route to do our share of the Beira patrol having refuelled at Gan on the way. Beira Patrol was an extremely boring task where we spent weeks just going up and down off the African coast. We would break the monotony by going into Mombassa to refuel/water/food/mail. One of the few interesting events of the patrol was the presence of a Portuguese frigate. It was their job to ensure we didn't encroach the 12-mile limit. They were as bored as we were, so we would sometimes break the boredom in the evening by holding inter-ship quizzes over the radio, it was all very friendly."

Salisbury arrived on 19 September at Aden, but only stayed overnight before starting in the direction of the Suez Canal at the other end of the Red Sea. She arrived at

Port Suez on 24 September. While in the Bitter Lakes in the Suez Canal *Salisbury's* double bottom plating sprang leaks and had to be 'corked' with quick setting concrete

Salisbury crossed the Mediterranean, with visits to Malta and Gibraltar. On 5 October she arrived at Falmouth where she anchored overnight before sailing into Devonport the following morning. On her return to Devonport there was a conference held onboard the frigate to decide whether the ship should be scrapped as a result of the bottom corrosion. Eventually, the decision was taken to repair the ship and return her to full commission.

After a brief visit to Portsmouth, *Salisbury* took part in *Exercise 'Rodean'* in the north Western Approaches in November that included *Hermes, Tiger, Berwick, Dido, Naiad, Phoebe, Russell, Salisbury, Olna* and *Retainer*. It was also an ASW exercise in the waters off Londonderry and the Canadian ships *Assinibone, Margaree, Chaudiere* and *Ottawa* joined in during some bad weather. *Salisbury* returned to her homeport of Devonport on 18 November.

Allan 'Buster' Brown remembers that *Salisbury* was in the United Kingdom for Christmas and New Year. "We sailed early in the New Year to relieve *Zest* as Bahamas guardship. The hand over took place at Bermuda. We visited Bermuda, Bahamas, Antigua, St Kitts and Anguilla in February. *Salisbury* landed four police officers from St Kitts on the island of Anguilla where there were disturbances on February 4 1967". *Exercise Winter Sun* in the Bahamas area took place from 2 March until 9 March 1967. *Salisbury* arrived at Houston on 14 March.

Allan 'Buster' Brown recalls the visit. "Our visit to Houston became particularly popular with crew and locals. As is often the tradition we held a party onboard for the orphans and less advantaged children of the city. For the party half of the ships crew dressed up as pirates whilst the other half befriended the children. The whole thing was covered by local television and thoroughly impressed the local population who took the ship to their hearts. Local people queued on the jetty in their cars hoping to entice members of the ship's crew away for winning and dining (commonly known in the RN as 'grippos'). I will never forget my hosts – amongst the Cadillacs and Chevrolets they arrived in what I swear was probably the only Triumph Herald in Texas, complete with a revolver in the glove compartment. Another event I recall from Houston was the example shown by one of my fellow communicators, Leading Radio Operator (LRO) Eddy Calvert. The ship opened to visitors on a couple of days and on the first day Eddy opened a 'real English Tea' stand on the forecastle. It was so popular Eddy was soon scouring the ship for tea. I don't know how much Eddy made but there wasn't much tea left onboard before the First Lieutenant found out what was going on and intervened."

After a brief visit to the beautiful island of Cayman Brac, *Salisbury* arrived at Montego Bay on 24 March. At Montego Bay *Salisbury* was one end of the finishing line, which stretched between the Montego Bay Yacht Club and the ship for the completion of a major yacht race which took place annually from Miami to Jamaica. April also saw visits to Bermuda and on 29 April *Salisbury* arrived at Turks- Caicos. She left the beautiful island on 1 May for an overnight passage to Great Inagua. Each destination was always just a day away and this continued when she visited Cuba on May 3 and the frigate operated off Guantanamo and also embarked S.N.O.W.I.

It was around this time that the ship would occasionally pick up 'boat people' trying to escape from Cuba. Some of who had been at sea for weeks with basic provisions. *Salisbury* would rescue them only to hand them over to the US Coastguard, who promptly sent them back to Cuba!

In between port visits, *Salisbury* continued the Bahama's Patrol and looked out for smugglers and illegal immigrants. Mid May the frigate visited Antigua and Carriacon before arriving at Roosevelt on 23 May 1967. It was then onto San Juan, Tortok and St Croix towards the end of the month. June continued in a similar fashion with ports of call paid to St Thomas, St Kitts, Antigua, St Lucia, Barbados before crossing the North Atlantic and calling at Ponta Delgada, where *Salisbury* refuelled. After this the frigate was called in to assist with the destruction of a dangerous ship, which had broken up after a storm.

The nuclear submarine *Dreadnought* had tried to destroy the forepart of the German chemical tanker *Essberger Chemist,* which had broken in two. She was carrying a cargo of ethanol and acetone. *Essberger Chemist* broke in two 90 miles south of the Azores on 2 June and was abandoned by her crew. The after part was towed to Punta Delgada on 5 June and subsequently towed to Piraeus before being sold to Spanish ship-breakers. The forepart arrived off the Azores on 8 June becoming a hazard to shipping. Despite being hit by torpedoes fired by *Dreadnought*, the hulk remained afloat because so many compartments remained intact. Consequently, *Salisbury* finally sank the wrecked forepart on 24 June using a number of 4.5-inch shells.

Upon her eventual return to Devonport on 28 June *Salisbury* was soon afterwards taken in hand for a major refit. Lieutenant (E) A R G Simmons took command of *Salisbury* on 28 October 1968. Almost a year later on 6 October 1969 another change of command took place, with the appointment of Commander I F Grant to the captain's chair.

In April 1970 *Salisbury* finally completed a two and a half year modernisation during which her lattice foremast was plated and her radar suite and AA armament was brought up to date. Thus, the ageing Types 293Q and 974 radars were replaced by Type 993 and 978 respectively. Furthermore, the Mk 5 40mm gun mounting aft was replaced by a quad launcher for SeaCat (GWS20) surface to air missiles with its director mounted on the after superstructure which had been further enlarged. Finally, single 20mm Oerlikon guns were fitted on either beam abreast the bridge and multiple rocket launchers for the Knebworth/Corvus chaff decoy system installed to port and starboard.

In April 1970 *Salisbury* was re-commissioned for service in the Western Fleet, which had replaced the Home Fleet. She spent the summer months working up at Portland and arrived at Portsmouth on 9 July. Two days later she sailed to take part in her first post refit exercise in the North Sea and East Atlantic under the auspices of NATO. The exercises finished when the participating warships visited the port of Leith on 16 July. *Salisbury* stayed alongside overnight before sailing south for Devonport, where she arrived on 19 July.

On 12 August 1970 *Salisbury* sailed from Devonport for Gibraltar, where upon her arrival she assumed the role of Gibraltar guardship until 7 September. Seven days later the frigate took part in the major *Exercise Northern Wedding* with some 180 ships including RN warships *Cavalier, Ark Royal, Britannia, Andromeda, Yarmouth, Aeneas*

21

and *Walrus* that finished on 26 September. September also saw port visits being made to Oporto, Den Helder and Stavanger. The following two months were spent operating in British waters preparing the crew and ship for her next Indian Ocean deployment in support of the Beira patrol.

On 9 November she left Devonport with *Puma*. The pair arrived at Gibraltar after six days at sea. Two days were spent at the Rock before the ships again headed to Simonstown, which was the next port of call on 2 December. At Simonstown, the Royal Navy sailors were challenged to a series of social and sporting activities and at all, the British seaman gave a good account of themselves against local teams. On 9 December *Salisbury* left to join the Far East Fleet, but not before she spent some time on the Beira patrol and at Mombassa. Indeed, *Salisbury* was on this patrol throughout Christmas and the New Year and it was only on 22 January 1971 that she was released so that she could sail for Singapore. After brief calls at Farquhar and Gan, *Salisbury* sailed into the Naval Dockyard on 4 February and stayed for just three days.

A three-week rest period was planned for the ship and crew at Hong Kong and upon the frigate's arrival, the ship's crew certainly started to enjoy their relaxation time. A number of the crew's wives joined the men-folk at the colony, whilst others explored the various delights on offer at Hong Kong.

On 8 March 1971 *Salisbury* left Hong Kong to start a short tour of Japanese ports. The first landfall was at Okinawa, which was followed by Yokohama and a return visit to Okinawa on 22 March. This visit was to undertake her duty in *PX.43*, which concluded at Manila Bay at the start of a SEATO exercise. She left the Philippines on 8 April and headed for Pulau Tioman, where some R and R was taken. Next port of call was Bangkok and then Hong Kong as a member of the 1st Far East Destroyer Squadron with the frigates *Scylla*, *Argonaut, Jaguar* and *Ghurka* on 24 April.

24 April 1971 also the arrival onboard *Salisbury* of another new commanding officer take up his position onboard the frigate. Commander R McQueen. She remained alongside until 10 May, when she slipped and made her way back to Singapore. The remainder of May was spent shuttling between Singapore and Hong Kong.

May and June the frigate was operating in the Singapore area before making a visit to Hong Kong and a return to Singapore at the end of July. Later in the month *Salisbury* put to sea to conduct exercises in the Malacca Strait with the aircraft carrier *Eagle* after which she sailed to Fremantle in Australia. The welcome the frigate received at the Australian port was fantastic and left many amongst the crew sad when *Salisbury* had to leave to rejoin the Beira Patrol.

On 8 June she arrived back at Singapore to start a maintenance period, which finished on 3 July. This maintenance was in order to prepare the ship for the voyage back to the United Kingdom, which started with a six-day courtesy visit to Fremantle on 14 July. *Salisbury* was to undertake another Beira Patrol upon her arrival off the East African coast, but before arriving there she visited Mauritius on 29 July. The Beira Patrol started on 1 August and for the next thirty days she tracked, monitored and occasionally intercepted shipping off Beira in order to en-force the oil embargo.

On 3 September *Salisbury* arrived at Simonstown and spent the next seven days preparing for the northward passage up Africa's West Coast before arriving at Gibraltar on 24 September. Having spent three days there she slipped and sailed for Devonport, where she arrived on 30 September. Soon after her arrival, *Salisbury* was docked within the dockyard until 8 November in order to carry out essential maintenance.

Salisbury arrived on 12 November at Portsmouth, before retracing her course to Devonport. On 22 November she left the West Country Naval Base for the Clyde, where she started to prepare for *Exercise Highwood* that would last until 9 December. The exercise was undertaken in Northern waters in early December in conditions varying from Force 10 to calm sunshine

On 9 December the ships refuelled at sea off the Firth of Forth and then set a course south to arrive at Portsmouth the next day. As the ships arrived at midday spectators lined the shoreline to welcome the warships back into port. Their arrival was something to witness as it had been quite sometime since seven Royal Navy warships arrived in line ahead. *Salisbury* brought up the rear after *London, Norfolk, Antrim, Ashanti, Hermione,* and *Naiad.*

1972 would prove to be a very active and busy time for *Salisbury*, after some initial weapon training at the beginning of January, the frigate carried out fishery patrols whilst operating out of Rosyth. January saw visits to Tromso, Bergen and Bodo before returning to Rosyth on 2 February. She stayed overnight before sailing for Devonport, where she spent the remainder of the month.

After calling at Portland, *Salisbury* was detailed to act as Gibraltar guard-ship until 27 March, before again returning to Guzz. April and May were a delight for many amongst the 200 men onboard, as the ship would visit a large number of British and European ports. Late April was spent in the Clyde, whilst between 4 and 9 May along with the frigate *Scylla*, *Salisbury* visited the French port of Rouen.

After a brief overnight stay at Portsmouth, *Salisbury* continued her tour of British ports with five days at Southampton, four at Dover and six-days at Falmouth. On 26 May 1972 *Salisbury* arrived back at Devonport. She carried out maintenance until 12 June, when she slipped and headed north for the Clyde areas, where she carried out a series of exercises, with amongst other Royal Navy ships, the aircraft carrier *Ark Royal* until the beginning of July.

On 19 July *Salisbury* had sailed south in order to visit Algiers for a five-day visit, before again taking on the role of Gibraltar guard-ship until 5 August. Three days later she arrived at Devonport and was opened to the public later in the month at that year's Navy Days. On 4 September she was taken to Chatham Dockyard to enter into the reserve fleet and to enter Preservation by Operation. She sailed into Chatham Dockyard one day after leaving Plymouth.

The following year a refit was commenced at Chatham but the Dockyard decided that they couldn't or wouldn't do the job and the frigate was towed to Devonport to refit. This took the whole of 1973 to complete. On 8 January 1974 Commander F N Ponsonby was appointed as the frigates latest commanding officer. Much work was still needed on the frigate and it was not until July that the ship was re-commissioned, even then there was still plenty of work for the dockyard to complete before the ship started her trials.

Over the August Bank Holiday weekend, *Salisbury* was opened to the public again at Plymouth Navy Days. Whilst in October 1974 *Salisbury* was taken in hand for six months of trials and work-up. In December the frigate operated in British waters and continued to work up with the 1st Frigate Squadron. The first few months of 1975 continued in the same vein, with a lengthy period of time spent at Devonport, before arriving at Gibraltar en route to the Beira patrol on 18 April. Calls were made to Bathurst, Banjul, Freetown and Lagos before she commenced her stint on the Beira patrol on 21 May.

In late May *Salisbury* arrived at Mombassa just after Mozambique had become independent to be told that their recent Beira patrol would be the last ever and that *Salisbury* would therefore not be resuming her Beira patrol duties on completion of an assisted maintenance period at Mombassa. Subsequently she sailed for the Seychelles.

The boredom of the Beira patrol gave way to much more pleasurable pursuits when in the summer of 1975 *Salisbury* visited a large variety of tropical and exotic destinations including the Seychelles, Mauritius, and Bombay. In August the frigate sailed to Colombo, a return visit to the Seychelles and after transiting the Suez Canal, she called at Malta.

On 1 September she left Malta and after three days steaming arrived at Gibraltar, where the ship was visited by the First Sea Lord, Admiral Sir Edward Ashmore who toured the ship. *Salisbury* arrived back at Devonport on 11 September, where she was docked for an extended maintenance period. The frigate only left dock on 24 October for initial trials. Seven days later she arrived at Portsmouth. Three days later she slipped and sailed for Portland.

On 6 November 1975 Commander H M White became the frigates' latest commanding officer while at Portland. On 30 November *Salisbury* sailed from Portland to Devonport. Almost two weeks later the frigate slipped out of the dockyard and into the River Tamar and out into Plymouth Sound. *Salisbury* arrived at Gibraltar to assume the role of guard-ship over Christmas. She left the Rock on 9 January 1976 and set a course for Malta. In the following fortnight, the frigate continued a mini-tour of the Mediterranean with visits to Livorno and Toulon. The visit to Livorno in Italy gave the crew the opportunity to visit Pisa, Florence and Lusca. Another incident of note was the rescue of a 600-ton coaster in the Mediterranean, with the assistance of RAF Nimrod aircraft. The *Katerina* was located, boarded and towed back to Malta, which the frigate had been visiting. Her stay in Livorno was, however, interrupted by fighting in Beirut and she was ordered to assist in the evacuation of UK nationals, however a ceasefire took place while *Salisbury* was off Cyprus and she sailed for Gibraltar.

Back at Devonport, the Mayor of the city of Salisbury visited *Salisbury*. In February the frigate operated off the British Isles and later off Iceland, in order to protect British trawlers during the Cod War. *Salisbury* spent four weeks on fisheries patrol off Iceland and suffered seven collisions. On 1 April her port side was hit by the stern of the Icelandic gunboat *Tyr* causing slight damage to both ships off the East Coast of Iceland.

April and May was spent in British waters, but the following two months were again spent off Iceland. The frigate suffered two more collisions in one day, this time with the Icelandic gunboat *Aegir* on 20 May during attempts to cut the warps of a group of trawlers.

The rest of 1976 was spent in safer pursuits with exercises and friendly port visits. She visited the French port of Calais in June and later in the summer was opened to the public for that year's Plymouth Navy Days held on 22 August. After more exercises *Salisbury* visited Amsterdam in September and Brest in November. In December the frigate was back at Devonport where Christmas leave was granted.

From January to March, *Salisbury* was in dockyard hands for an extended docking period at Devonport to remove Cod War dents and bruises inflicted by the Icelandic vessels. Lieutenant Commander J T Sanders became *Salisbury's* final Commanding Officer on 11 January 1977.

Once finally completely repaired *Salisbury* slipped from Devonport on 4 April and sailed for Portland to work up. Another milestone was marked on 28 April when *Salisbury* fired the very last squid AS mortar Mk4 weapon in Royal Navy service. It should have been a pattern of three but two failed to leave the barrels. The squid and associated Sonar's were subsequently removed from the ship during another period in Devonport in May.

The Queen's Silver Jubilee brought together a large number of warships from around the world to celebrate the Queen's twenty-five years on the British throne. *Salisbury* was one of the British ships attending the event held in Spithead. *Salisbury* was positioned between *Apollo* and *Gurkha*. Following the success of the event, the frigate left soon after to Devonport to repair a faulty generator.

In Mid July, *Salisbury* left Devonport for a one month stint as Gibraltar guardship, upon her return to Plymouth, the frigate was opened to the public at Devonport Navy Days held over the late August Bank holidays. During the show *Salisbury* was moored inboard of the frigate *Euryalus*. Also during August, an interesting event occurred onboard the ship. Members of the Naval Provost Marshall staff at HMS *Drake* took part in filming for an HTV production called *'The Doombolt Chase'* which also involved *Salisbury*.

Having returned to sea in September, *Salisbury* resumed her duties in connection with protecting British interests in the Economic Exclusion Zones and on fishery patrols. During this patrol, *Salisbury* went to the assistance of *RFA Blue Rover*, who had lost her rudder off Bergen, and escorted her and her tugs to Rosyth. By mid October *Salisbury* returned to Devonport Dockyard for treatment for a vibration in her port shaft.

In December she was heavily employed in United Kingdom waters and visited Portland and Faslane. When she arrived off Plymouth on Christmas Eve the crew were busy preparing for some well earned leave, but instead were ordered to assist a Greek freighter, which had run into trouble in Carmarthen Bay. *Salisbury* continued up the Irish Sea and eventually refuelled at Faslane on Christmas Day.

On Boxing Day *Salisbury* was at sea when she was detailed to shadow the huge Russian aircraft carrier *Kiev*. She maintained a presence on the massive ship for the next three days and her photographic department took a-great many photographs that would be scrutinised by intelligence personnel. Following this interesting incident, *Salisbury* returned to Devonport, where leave was granted.

1978 was as busy as any year in *Salisbury's* long career. The frigate conducted a series of exercises in February as part of a Joint Maritime Course. The following month, *Salisbury* sailed to Gibraltar for a month long stint as Gibraltar guard-ship. During this period, at Midnight on Easter Day, *Salisbury* left the port to shadow the Russian hybrid aircraft carrier/cruiser *Kiev* again. In April *Salisbury* returned to Devonport after calling at Lisbon.

Following a port visit to Southampton on June 14 *Salisbury* returned to Devonport to pay off into reserve. Later that year she was sold to Egypt and had actually sailed as far as Gibraltar on her delivery voyage before the deal was cancelled and she had to return to the United Kingdom.

In 1980 *Salisbury* became a static sea training ship for Raleigh and was moored in the River Tamar replacing *Ulster* in the role. For the next five years *Salisbury* filled this important task but was ultimately replaced by the Leander class frigate *Ajax*. On 14 September 1985 *Salisbury* was towed from Plymouth for use as a target. Sixteen days later she was sunk 300 miles west of Ireland; a number of weapons were fired at her including laser guided bombs from an RAF Buccaneer strike aircraft and a Harpoon missile from a Nimrod aircraft. A Sub Harpoon missile from *Trafalgar*, was, however credited with the final kill.

LEOPARD

Construction of the name ship of the Type 41 class frigates began on March 25 1953, when the first steel plates were laid down at Portsmouth Dockyard. Just over two years later on May 23 1955 Her Highness Princess Marie Louise launched the frigate. The pace of her construction slowed somewhat after that and it wouldn't be until 30 September 1958 that *Leopard* was commissioned at Portsmouth Dockyard. The next day saw the appointment of Commander R G Gaunt DSC as the frigate's first commanding officer.

Commander Gaunt had spent his childhood in South Africa and had joined the RNVRSA before becoming a seaman gunner in *Winchester Castle*. Robert Gaunt travelled to the United Kingdom for officer training and after passing out joined the Royal Navy's coastal forces and served on *MTB 222* and *MTB 223*. Whilst onboard *MTB 237* he saw action at night when the British force engaged eleven German warships. In the ensuing battle his boat was sunk. Later Gaunt transferred to the 9th MTB flotilla at Dartmouth and onboard *MTB231* saw action off the Channel Islands. His talent was noted and for a brief period he was XO of *MTB 640* before being posted to India as commanding officer of *MTB283* in the 17th MTB flotilla.

Having returned to the United Kingdom, he was in charge of *MTB254* during a convoy action off Le Harve. Later he was appointed as executive officer of *Grey Fox* during sweeping operations for Oyster Mines off the French coast.

In December 1958 *Leopard* joined the 7th Frigate Squadron Home and South Atlantic. The frigate, however, continued to work up around Portland until 8 May 1959. Having spent the next twenty-days at Portsmouth, *Leopard* left to take up South African and South American station duties. *Leopard* stopped over at Gibraltar before visiting Abidjan on 15 June. At Abidjan the frigate and crew were given a farewell gift of fruit from the African deputy Prime Minister. Next port of call was at Lagos where the frigate arrived on 20 June. There after the usual official niceties had been carried out, the crew entertained a group of local children during a party onboard the frigate. Then it was onto Port Harcourt. To enter the port the frigate had to travel forty-one miles along the Bonny River with mangrove swamps on either beam. When she visited Calabar on 28 June, *Leopard* was visited the by Governor of Eastern Nigeria, Sir Robert de Stapledon. After three days *Leopard* sailed from the port.

On 3 July 1959 *Leopard* arrived at Lagos for a ten-day maintenance period. Once prepared for the Trans-Atlantic crossing to South America *Leopard* left the port on 13 July to visit Rio de Janeiro with *Lynx, Chichester* and the aircraft carrier *Albion*. She remained in South American waters until 3 August when she again crossed the South Atlantic to arrive at Simonstown on 21 August.

The autumn of 1959 was spent conducting exercises and the usual round of official visits. On 5 November she arrived at Make in the Seychelles Island chain. Remaining in the area for the whole of the month, she also visited the island of Agalega, before arriving at Mauritius on 28 November. Ten days were spent enjoying the hospitality of the locals before *Leopard* sailed back to Simonstown arriving at the naval base on 15 December.

Two days later the frigate left and sailed to Capetown for a short two-day visit before returning to Simonstown. There she entered dry-dock and whilst the crew enjoyed Christmas and New Year ashore, the ship received much needed attention until 1 March 1960.

Within six hours of leaving Simonstown on March 1 for a South American cruise, en route to the UK, *Leopard* was recalled and despatched to Durban to stand by in case she was needed to carry supplies and render aid to the cyclone stricken island of Mauritius. Whilst on passage to Durban, plans were laid to embark and stow 100 tons of stores and to land and man two field kitchens each capable of serving 1,500 meals a day, but on March 5 the island's authorities decided *Leopard's* aid would not be needed. Next morning the ship, left Durban, her unexpected third visit there and after a three-hour stop in Simonstown on March 8 resumed her interrupted cruise.

The twelve day passage to the Falklands was uneventful and the weather kind. After two days in Port Stanley, *Leopard* left on March 22 and rendezvoused with Ice Patrol Ship *Protector* before continuing westwards to enter the Straits of Magellan and arrive at

Puntus Arenas. Her stay was short and early on 26 March she continued through the straits as far as Cape Froward, the southern most point of South America.

At midday she turned south to enter the Magdalena Channel and follow the torturous route through the little known waterways of the Tierra del Fuego.

A South Westerly course was chosen to take *Leopard* through the Cockburn Channel; but the force of the Pacific swell took the crew by surprise as the ship turned to the South East to enter the narrow Brecknock Pass. Those who could spare the time could see ice capped mountains from portholes and windows on the bridge.

Leopard continued her journey across the comparatively open waters of Desolate Bay and Whaleboat Sound before anchoring for the night in a sheltered bay among the Londonderry islands. The next morning *Leopard* sailed through the O'Brien Channel towards the North West arm of the Beagle Channel. Again the sight of huge, towering cliff faces of glaciers fascinated the crew of the frigate, especially as the closest of them were a mere 400 yards from the ship. That afternoon the frigate berthed at Ushuaia, then a small Argentinean Naval base. Ushuania is the southern most Town in the world and as such lacked a great deal of the creature comforts but the welcome from the Argentineans was warm and genuine. *Leopard* sailed on March 29 to retrace at high speed her passage through to Puntus Arenas.

After anchoring overnight off Puntus Arenas, *Leopard* left the Straits of Magellan and entered the South Atlantic and continued up the East Coast of South America. Her first point of call was at Puerto Madryn on the Golfo Nuevo. The town had only rarely seen a Royal Navy warship, the last having been twenty five years earlier when the cruiser *Delhi* visited in 1935. Then it was onto another Argentine naval base, this time Mar del Plata, where submarines were based. There were also excellent breaks near the town, which the crew enjoyed. On April 14 *Leopard* left Argentina and sailed north for Brazil and the fascinating city of Rio de Janeiro four days later.

On April 21 the new city of Brasilia was inaugurated as the new capital of the United States of Brazil and *Leopard* had the distinction of being the only foreign warship present at Rio on this historic occasion. *Leopard* left Rio the next day to explore the

Amazon Rain Forest. The heat and humidity was intense as she arrived at Belem, capital of the state of Para on 29 April.

Within twenty-four hours she was again under way and following an intricate course through the maze of islands. Next morning the channel in which *Leopard* was navigating was in places just 200 yards wide making the jungle seem very close indeed. On May 2 1960 *Leopard* anchored, for a couple of hours in the dogwatch, off the colourful little town of Obidos. The Amazonian adventure, however, continued as the frigate continued up the world's longest river. She sailed up the river for three days until on May 5 she anchored off the village of Codajas, 1,144 miles from the mouth of the river. This was the furthest upstream that any Royal Navy warship had gone since the survey ship *Pelorus* in 1909.

Leopard's unscheduled visit to Codajas proved to be timely as upon her arrival her crew discovered that the village had been cut off owing to the high level of the river. Furthermore a shortage of food and water led to cases of Malaria and dysentery. Medical supplies and food were distributed before the ship turned around to start her return journey. Next afternoon, *Leopard* berthed at Manaus, the big port a few miles up the Rio Negro river and stayed there two days before continuing her swift downward passage. The only other port of call was at Santarem for a couple of hours. After a night at Belem, *Leopard* returned to the open sea. She crossed the Atlantic and the equator to arrive at Gibraltar, where she arrived on 23 May. At Gibraltar *Leopard* transferred from the South African and South Atlantic Station to the Home Fleet. On May 27 *Leopard* finally arrived home at Portsmouth and soon after entered into refit, which took up the summer months of 1960. *Leopard* returned to the active fleet on 23 September.

She left port on 15 October and started a period of trials in the Solent and English Channel. Acting as the cruiser *Blake's* guardship, *Leopard* arrived in Northern Irish waters. It was in these waters that *Leopard* was involved in a maritime rescue operation. *Leopard* and helicopters of 719 squadron from RNAS Eglington worked in very adverse weather conditions to rescue nearly 30 members of the crew of the Greek cargo ship *Argo Delos*, which went aground off the Donegal coast on October 22 1960. Although the master was taken off he insisted upon returning to his ship and stayed onboard until October 25 when a helicopter delivered a note from the owners instructing him to leave the battered ship. Following this rescue the Captain and Lieutenant Anthony-Neville Graham Smith , were amongst a number of the crew who received the silver medal from the Greek ambassador.

Leopard returned to Portsmouth on 28 October, and three days later Commander P.S. Hicks-Beach became the frigate's new commanding officer. On 3 November *Leopard* left Portsmouth and again headed north to Londonderry. Later in the month she visited Swansea before returning to Portsmouth on the first day of December.

The frigate remained at Portsmouth throughout the winter months and ventured to sea next on 4 April 1961, when she sailed to Gibraltar en route to her SASA station at Simonstown. En route *Leopard* paid a four-day visit to Bathurst, before sailing onto Freetown in Sierra Leone. The visit was organised to celebrate Sierra Leone's independence. Other Royal Navy ships there for the ceremony included the cruiser *Bermuda* and *Lynx*, whilst the America's provided *USS Hermitage*, *Nigeria* came from Nigeria and *Afadzato* came from Ghana.

May 1961 saw port visits to Tema, Lagos, Luanda and on 22 May *Leopard* finally arrived at Simonstown. The following month would see the frigate paying official ports of call, to Capetown and courtesy calls to the island of St Helena in the middle of the South Atlantic. *Leopard* dropped off supplies to the inhabitants of the desolate island and medical personnel onboard the frigate dealt with any medical concerns, before returning to Simonstown on 21 June.

Leopard slipped on 3 July and visited Port Elizabeth, East London and Durban before entering Mombassa on 24 July. She entered the Indian Ocean to visit Diego Suarez and Mauritius before again returning to Simonstown. In September *Leopard* participated in six weeks of intensive exercises with local naval forces in *CAPEX*. Also included in the force was sister-ship *Jaguar*. The exercises started on 27 September. Half way through these exercises, however, a natural disaster called the frigate away.

Leopard had entered Simonstown harbour on the evening of October 9, to disembark her flight of Pilotless Target aircraft prior to sailing for an operational visit to

Hermanus, about 100 miles west of the naval base. As she passed the breakwater on the way out at about 1800, a signal was received stating that there was an emergency in Tristan du Cunha and ordering the ship to remain alongside.

At 2000 *Leopard* filled her fuel tanks to capacity and stood by to receive 16 tons of emergency stores. Two hours later the signal was received to load the stores as quickly as possible. Talk amongst the crew confirmed that the destination was the island of Tristan da Cunha and the reason was a massive volcanic eruption.

The 16 tons of stores ranged from blankets to six inch nails and tarpaulins to split peas, were loaded in just under four hours. *Leopard* sailed at 04.00 and set a course for the island in the middle of the South Atlantic. The weather conditions were not good as the 1,600 miles were covered in three and a half days. When the frigate neared the island the islanders told the frigate over the radio of continuing tremors which had caused rock falls and cracks in the roads and pavements of the island. All day on the 9 October, the cracks continued until the volcano erupted on the 10 October and began to increase in size rapidly; by that evening it was 100 feet high!

By the afternoon of October 12, the island had been evacuated of all 257 inhabitants and had been taken onboard the Dutch liner *Tjisadane* on their way to Cape Town. The Administrator of the island, Mr Peter Wheeler, was aboard the *Tristania*; a 600-ton fishing vessel attached to the cannary on the island.

Leopard's task was to salvage valuable and personal belongings, to embark the heavy gear from the Canning Factory and to destroy the islands dog population. *Leopard* arrived off Tristan da Cunha at 1000 on Friday 13 October and rounded the northern tip of the island and shaped course for the anchorage at midday on Friday October 13.

There were eight landing parties each of three men, to go round the crofts collecting as much personal gear as possible, a party of three armed with rifles to destroy dogs and a skilled technical party to remove valuable equipment. All the parties were controlled by the headquarters section that were, in turn, in contact with the embarkation beach and the ship by radio and signal lamp.

The task of destroying the island's dogs was perhaps the hardest task of all. The dogs were unfortunately not going with their owners and had to be destroyed for their own good. Still those sailors who had to shoot them found the task an unpleasant one. The original plan had been to round up the dogs and shoot them through their heads as painlessly as possible. Unfortunately, after the first few had been dispatched, the dogs became timid and would not come near the party. It was found that the .22 rifles were not sufficient to kill a dog outright. The marksmen returned to the ship and the next day brought 303 rifles to complete the task.

The race to complete the evacuation was completed and as night fell *Leopard* sailed. The islanders took a last look at the glowing volcano where the rocks were now reaching the path down to the canning factory and getting close to the first cottages.

The trip back to Cape Town was made more interesting by the crew's efforts to raise a fund for the islanders so that they would have some spending money on their trip to the United Kingdom. Collecting boxes were placed around the ship, at the entry to the cinema shows, at beer issues and the contributions from the daily tombola sessions were also donated.

There was also a mammoth raffle held onboard, with prizes ranging from Transistor radios to three months of free haircuts. The draw was conducted by the Captain and Mr Wheeler and took place at sea shortly before the frigate arrived at Cape Town. When the total in the fund had been counted, it was £235. At Capetown the passengers were unloaded along with trucks and cases of supplies.

Ten days after leaving *Leopard* returned to Simonstown. The ship spent a period in self-maintenance, which was completed on 3 December.

The next day she slipped to sea to begin her South American cruise arriving at Rio de Janeiro on 14 December. After three days ashore, the crew returned to the ship and then proceeded onto the next destination of the Argentinean Capital City of Buenos Aires. Christmas was a very special occasion in this very religious state and the crew of the British frigate were, welcomed into the celebrations ashore. *Leopard* sailed two days later for the port of Fray Bentos, the capital of the Rio Negro region of Uruguay. The city was founded in 1859 as Independencia and renamed for an 18th century religious hermit of the region. The meatpacking centre of South America was an interesting destination and the ship celebrated the New Year there before sailing later on 1 January.

The Argentinean Navy's naval base at Puerto Belgrano welcomed the ship with a great deal of hospitality. Social and sporting events occupied a large part of the three-days spent there, before *Leopard* continued her journey. January would also see visits paid to Talcahuano, Callao and on 29 January a transit of the Panama Canal and *Leopard* entered into the Atlantic Ocean.

On 31 January 1962 *Leopard* visited Cartagena before going onto visit Trinidad on 7 February. Nine days later, *Leopard* pulled into the port at Dakar. Five days were spent alongside, to allow the crew some leave and to affect some repairs to the ship before resuming her passage back to the United Kingdom.

On 26 February she arrived at Gibraltar and remained in the area in preparation for the annual *Exercise Dawn Breeze*. Most of March was spent carrying out exercises off Gibraltar with other Royal Navy units before leaving for home on 26 March. Four days later *Leopard* returned to Portsmouth and entered into refit. The modifications were completed on 2 August, and were followed by a period of trials. On 3 September Lieutenant Commander D C Griffiths assumed command.

On 24 September *Leopard* left Portsmouth to visit Cuxhaven before taking part in October's *43/60*. On 7 October *Leopard* was at Londonderry, which was followed by a few days spent at Greenock for FOS/M A1 and A2. The next few weeks were spent shuttling between Portland, Devonport and Portsmouth. Christmas and New Year were spent at Portsmouth, before resuming her training program at Portland in early 1963. To prepare the frigate for her next planned extended deployment she was taken into dock at Portsmouth for an inspection and repairs, this was completed on 22 March 1963. She was undocked that day and sailed later to Portland where her work up's were completed.

On 27 March *Leopard* arrived at Las Palmas on her passage south to South Africa. The following month saw the frigate visiting Sao Vicente, Dakar, Bathurst, Freetown in Sierra Leone and on 22 April Abidjan in Ghana. Ghana received a second visit from the frigate four days later when she arrived at Tema. *Leopard* then set a course south and spent the next three days at sea, before arriving at Lagos on the last day of April.

On 10 May *Leopard* finally arrived at Simonstown. The next fortnight was spent alongside, with the ship receiving maintenance and the crew enjoying a well-earned period of leave.

When she returned to sea on 25 May, *Leopard* entered the Indian Ocean and went onto visit Mauritius and Diego Suarez before returning to Simonstown. Eight days alongside ended on 25 June when the frigate slipped to sea. Her first port of call was to Walvis Bay, where the ships taking part in *CAPEX* started to assemble.

At the start of serial 801 at 02.30, in the early morning of 28 July, Blue Force consisted of the South African Algerine minesweeper *Pietermaritzburg*, carrying a valuable cargo. The minesweeper was on a base line course of 310 degrees, screened by *Transvaal* and *Good Hope* with *Leopard* representing a Tiger class cruiser formed astern of *Pietermaritzburg* at two and half cables.

Three hours later the 'enemy' was detected on the starboard bow and 'Action Stations' was sounded. At about 05.10 *Leopard* altered 10 degrees to the starboard to a course of 320 and then increased to 17 knots to haul out and overtake *Pietermaritzburg*. No signal was made to the South African warship or the other ships in Blue Force.

Star Shells were used to simulate an attack on *Transvaal*, when *Leopard's* First Lieutenant saw movement of the reflection of starshell on *Pietermaritzburg's* side. He immediately ordered 'Starboard 30. Stop both engines". Moments later the two ships struck one another at almost right angles. *Pietermaritzburg's* bow penetrated *Leopard's* port side between 3 and 7 stations. 18-year-old Able Seaman Thomas Bolton of Aberdeen was in the compartment and was killed.

Leopard made for Port Elizabeth, where initial assessments of the damage were undertaken before returning to Simonstown via Capetown. The damaged frigate arrived at Simonstown on 20 August and was soon docked to affect initial repairs to the damaged port bow that cost £886 (1963 prices). The work was completed in early September and *Leopard* was prepared for sea and the journey back home to the United Kingdom for permanent repairs. The frigate left Simonstown on 12 September and routed home via Freetown and Gibraltar, arriving at Portsmouth on 1 October.

The damaged bow was cut away and replaced with a new structure with the repairs being completed on 11 January 1964. The frigate seemed plagued with troubles as soon after being repaired her engines developed faults that prevented *Leopard* sailing to the Far East for a month. After trials and ensuing modifications *Leopard* finally sailed from Portsmouth on 26 February

Leopard was routed through the Mediterranean and paid calls at Gibraltar and Malta before transiting southwards through the Suez Canal. Next port of call was to Aden, where she spent a few hours refuelling before continuing her journey into the Indian Ocean. Late spring and summer was spent patrolling in the Persian Gulf and Far East with numerous and frequent opportunities to exercise with foreign navies and to share the Royal Navy's experience with these smaller navies. *Leopard's* crew willingly shared their knowledge and in turn learnt a great deal from these shared experiences. Almost all exercises ended with a port trip, where the locals challenged the visiting ships, such as *Leopard* to some healthy sporting competition. *Leopard's* crew won a good share of the matches they entered, but lost quite a few as well.

The humid and hot summer of the Gulf was left behind as the frigate returned to Portsmouth on 4 September 1964 to enter into an extensive refit, which would see the ship in dockyard hands until February 1966. Throughout the course of her refit command of the frigate was transferred to Lt (SD) (TAS) R P Fox, who assumed command on 8 January 1965.

After almost a year in refit on 4 December 1965 *Leopard's* command was again transferred to Commander J A D Ford. The frigate remained at Portsmouth until 1 August 1966. Three days later the frigate arrived at Gibraltar, before entering the Mediterranean en route to the Indian Ocean and the Far East. She was routed through Malta, The Suez Canal and Aden before arriving at Mombassa on 25 August. Self-maintenance was carried out until the end of the month and then she assumed patrols in the Mozambique Channel in support of the Beira Patrol, with breaks spent at Mombassa, until 4 October.

Six days later *Leopard* arrived at Gan and five days later slipped into harbour. The frigate took part in exercises at Singapore, Hong Kong and Manila, which culminated with *Leopard* taking the coveted Far East Fleet AA Gunnery Trophy. Christmas 1966 was spent at Bangkok. *Leopard* returned to the Beira Patrol when she returned to Mombassa. In fact, she visited the area several times during nine weeks on Beira patrol and on the last occasion Commander J A D Ford handed over command to Commander N R D King on 1 May 1967.

Commander King had been onboard only a week when on May 27 *Leopard* was ordered out of Mombassa for an unknown destination. This turned out to be Aden, where with *Hermes*, other frigates and a squadron of minesweepers the ship exercised and awaited the outcome of the latest Middle East crisis. Eventually the political tension died away and *Leopard* returned to the United Kingdom with the frigates *Cleopatra* and *Ashanti* via the Cape. Crossing the Equator King Neptune paid a call to initiate 18 'victims' who had joined the ship since leaving England. They were washed and dunked as punishment for numerous trumped up charges – all done in good fun mind.

The next stopover was to have been Gibraltar, but half way up the bulge of Africa a signal turned the ship about and sent her haring off for another secret destination, though not before prospective husbands and her few sick had been transferred to *Cleopatra*. Within twenty hours a distress call was heard from a Greek merchant ship just fifteen miles away. By the time she got there the ship had sunk and a Swedish ship had rescued the crew.

Leopard carried on her secret mission but when ERA Callard developed appendicitis the ship immediately made for Takoradi.

Shortly afterwards another signal was received ordering the ship to make for Freetown and Gibraltar and home. After customs inspections *Leopard* arrived at Portsmouth on July 22. She remained at Portsmouth throughout the summer months conducting repairs. On 20 November the ship sailed to cross the North Atlantic and assume the role of West Indies guardship.

First port of call was on 23 November when the frigate arrived at Ponta Delgada. Two days later she sailed onto Bermuda. The final port of call for November was reached on the last day of the month when *Leopard* arrived at Bermuda for a short visit. December proved to be a very busy month, with port visits to Antigua and Beef Island before assuming the Bermuda and Bahamas patrol. During the passage the frigate encountered some very heavy weather which made for a very slow, uncomfortable crossing. With Commodore J M Townley onboard the ship returned to the Bahama's for her first patrol whilst Christmas was spent at Freeport on Grand Bahama. During the following weeks three Cuban fishing boats apparently fishing within the Bahamian territorial waters were arrested.

Nassau was reached after dark on New Year's Eve just in time for Junkanoo – the Nassau New Year equivalent of carnival. The 60,000 inhabitants of Nassau, however, looked like having a somewhat dull Christmas and New Year until *Leopard* arrived. The electricity on the island was failing and *Leopard* connected her own generators to the shore network through a sub station on the jetty. For two days the ship provided the power to government offices and the centre of the town.

If anything January 1968 continued along a similar vein with a wide variety of patrol duties and an assortment of ports of call. The first was at Panama on 11 January, when she entered the canal and transited to the Pacific Ocean. After leaving Panama, the first port of call was at Acapulco on 20 January. The holiday resort of the rich and famous on Mexico's coast attracted the attention of the crew's sun seekers many choosing to spend some time on the world famous beaches. On 1 February, *Leopard* arrived at Punta Arenas for a series of exercises that concluded with the frigate's arrival back at the Canal area and a return to the Caribbean.

Leopard took part in 'Caribex' until 15 February 1968. The next day *Exercise Springboard* started and this in turn lasted until 17 February, when the participating warships all sailed into San Juan. Two days were spent taking part in social and sporting events with the other ships in the force but *Leopard* sailed for a maintenance period at Bermuda that occupied the crew and dockyard workers until mid March. *Leopard* resumed the Bahamian patrol, but did visit the American base at Key West for a week in late March.

On 2 April *Leopard* arrived at Kingston for a two-day visit before going onto visit Santa Domingo. The city had experienced a severe drought when the frigate arrived and strict water restrictions were in force. *Leopard* provided literally tons of fresh water from her tanks to the city. *Leopard* also took some members of the Dominican Navy to sea for sea training with the Royal Navy. The frigate visited Lascalderas and resumed the Bahamian patrol until the end of April. Again, the boredom of the patrol was broken with a visit to the island paradise of Nassau for three days between 12 and 15 April. This time the electricity on the island worked well and *Leopard* did not need to offer the use of her generators. On the last day of the visit *Leopard* slipped and also arrived at Freeport. On her return to sea another stint of patrol duties ended on 10 May when the crew visited Fort Lauderdale in Florida and many of them took the opportunity to visit the attractions of the sunshine state during the ships' four-day stay. The whole state of Florida was overwhelmed by the American-space-program and the increasing pace of the Apollo moon shots. Some of the crew visited Cape Kennedy Space Centre with the intention of maybe catching a rocket launch.

At Savannah in Georgia, a-children's party was organised and over 3000 people toured the ship when it was open to the public to view. After a call at Norfolk, *Leopard* was quickly sent back to Bermuda, following disturbances on the island and berthed at Hamilton. After nine days in the area and only when the situation ashore was under control did *Leopard* leave to arrive back at Portsmouth on 1 June.

During this time alongside, command of the frigate was transferred to Commander A D Hutton on 11 June and re-commissioned three days later. The maintenance period was concluded on 8 July. Two days later *Leopard* escorted the aircraft carrier *Hermes* as her plane guard in the English Channel, the frigate, however, was soon back at Portsmouth and was opened to the public for 1968's Navy Days. When she left Portsmouth on 5 September, she sailed to Portland to prepare for her participation in *Exercise Silver Tower*, held later in the month until 27 September, before returning to Portsmouth the next day.

She remained alongside until 21 October, when *Leopard* sailed for Gibraltar to spend the next two-months in the Mediterranean. *Leopard* called at Reggio at the end of October. She along with the frigate *Mohawk* arrived at the port, only to find it was a national holiday weekend and nothing was open. The Italian's seemed to forget that this visit was the first by a Royal Navy vessel, no less two, for over twelve years. The crew of the two frigates, however, enjoyed time on the golden beaches. *Leopard* returned to Gibraltar before taking part in the international exercise *Exercise Eden Apple* that started on 5 November. For the next fortnight the ships practised manoeuvres with one another in order to improve and enhance inter navy co-operation in the region. UK forces in the region were the destroyers *Hampshire* wearing the flag of Vice Admiral A M Lewis CB, Flag Officer Flotillas, Western Fleet, *Kent, Barossa* and *Cavalier* together with the frigates *Arethusa, Juno, Sirius, Mohawk, Zulu, Toubridge* and sister ship *Jaguar*. Below the waves a large RN submarine force was also present including *Valiant, Oracle, Osiris* and *Alliance*.

The exercises involved Buccaneer aircraft of 800 squadron, Sea Vixens from 899 squadron and 849D Gannet flight from the aircraft carrier *Eagle*, undergoing refit at Devonport at the time. The RAF flew out the squadron personnel and stores to the Italian Air Force Base at Decimomannu in Sardinia from where the Sea Vixens and Gannets operated and to the RAF base at Luqua on Malta for the Buccaneers.

During the opening days of the exercise the 50 ships taking part came under light air attack and were tracking enemy submarines in two areas of the Mediterranean. One group comprising of British, French and Italian surface ships including the French aircraft carrier *Foch*, exercised defence procedures, replenishment at sea and anti submarine warfare.

The other group, were engaged in surface and air gunnery operations against targets at Filfa Rock on Malta. Later in *Eden Apple*, the two groups combined and came under attack from missile armed patrol boats and anti-sabotage operations were carried out to defend against frogmen and mines.

The second phase of the exercise stepped up the anti somewhat, with large scale massed air attacks on the fleet whilst operating in the Ionian Sea and Tyrreenian Sea and the Straits of Sardinia. The attacks were carried out by aircraft from the Italian Air Force's 5th Tactical air force. Another group of vessels, simulating an amphibious force crossed the central Mediterranean to an area south of Greece near Kithera and came under further fast attack craft attack. The exercises came to an end on November 16 when many of the ships sailed to Naples.

On 22 November, *Leopard* sailed into Grand Harbour at Malta before arriving back at Gibraltar eight days later. After two days within the naval complex on the colony, *Leopard* returned to Portsmouth. Ten days later on 16 December the frigate was taken in hand for an extensive refit that would keep her out of commission until the end of 1969

The frigate's refit was due to complete 8 August 1969 after which she remained in the Portsmouth area conducting trials before sailing to the Channel Island on 23 August to visit St Helier. She returned to Portsmouth on 24 August, where over the late Bank Holiday weekend the frigate was open to the public during Navy Days.

Leopard was declared operational to the fleet from 12 September 1969 and in the next few weeks carried out her work up programme, in the waters around Portland in Dorset. A further period of maintenance was carried out at Portsmouth until 24 November to prepare the frigate for her lengthy period away, which started four days later when she left Portsmouth.

First port of call was on 29 November at Gibraltar before continuing her southerly journey via Freetown and Port Elizabeth where she arrived on 20 December. At Port Elizabeth many of the ships-company took a trip to the Addu National Park and also visited the local snake pits. Ten days later *Leopard* assumed the duties required of the Beira Patrol. The frigate remained at sea throughout the festive period and was only relieved on duty on 28 January. On the last day of January 1970, *Leopard* arrived at Mombassa where she was met by the Kenyan Navy's patrol boat Chui. Chui in Swahali means Leopard and after the two vessels exchanged crests and photographs were taken.

One day before Valentine's Day, *Leopard* left Mombassa following a period of maintenance to resume her Beira Patrol duties that occupied the crew until mid March. The frigate then sailed in the direction of Singapore and arrived at the base on 23 March. It was a very short stay of just one-day, before *Leopard* sailed for Hong Kong, where repairs to the ship were undertaken. These were completed on 25 May when *Leopard* left to take part in *Exercise Crackshot* that lasted until 5 June when she returned to Singapore. After ten days alongside she took part in *Exercise Matlock*, a twenty-day exercise to test the Royal Navy and other navies in the region. At the end of the exercise *Leopard* returned to Singapore, where she remained until late July. In August *Leopard* was moved to a floating dock in Sebawang shipyard. *Leopard* received her new direction finding aerial by courtesy of helicopters of 847 NAS. This was the first time a frigate in Singapore has had an aerial delivered by helicopter. The operation took less than 10 minutes to complete, much quicker than by crane.

By 3 August *Leopard* arrived at Hong Kong for a two-day stop over en route to Maizuru in Japan. The visit to the Japanese port was a huge success and after five days a great many new friends had been made between the ship and the port. A similar reception greeted *Leopard* when she arrived at the next port on the itinerary, Kagoshima on 14 August. Her arrival, however, had been delayed by forty-eight hours due to the circumnavigation of a typhoon that gave the ship something of a bouncy ride before her arrival at Kagoshima on Japan's southern tip. She also visited Kyototo where a few of the crew took advantage of an offer to visit Expo in Osaka.

Leopard's route home to the United Kingdom was via the so called 'Rich man's route' across the Pacific, via Midway and Pearl Harbor in Hawaii. *Leopard's* crew enjoyed four days at Pearl Harbor where during off duty times, some of the crew tried their hand at surf boarding in the world famous waters of the islands.

After a seven day passage from Pearl Harbor the ship reached Esquimalt in Canada for an assisted maintenance period. Ratings from the warship were scattered all over Vancouver Island, some spending their weekend in tents, log cabins, farms, flats and boats whilst Chief Petty Officer's gave a reception for their Canadian opposite numbers and their wives. *Leopard* was also opened to the public and around 4000 people visited the ship during a weekend. *Leopard* later steamed up the Columbia River to Portland, Oregon, where there was a party on board for orphans in the American city.

On 23 September the frigate arrived at San Francisco where one of the best attractions was said to be a plentiful supply of British beer. Seven days were spent alongside before slipping to sea and sailing south towards the huge American naval base at San Diego. During her time in San Diego, *Leopard's* crew were granted leave and they chose a variety of destinations. The crew chose from Dallas, Los Angeles, Disneyland, Las Vegas, Mexico and San Francisco. All enjoyed the time away from the ship, especially the few who made money at Las Vegas. With the crew back onboard the frigate, she put to sea to take part in a series of exercises and arranged shoots that had been organised by the US Navy and Canadian Armed Forces.

On 6 October 1970 *Leopard* left San Diego and sailed south to arrive at Manzanillo three days later. After a brief visit to Bilboa, *Leopard* arrived at Colon on 17 October before passing through the Panama Canal and into the Caribbean. Two days later *Leopard* reached the Guantanamo exercise areas, where she operated with American warships in the area before sailing onto Bermuda. On the last day of October the frigate reached Ponta Delgada for a one day visit.

Leopard returned to Portsmouth on 5 November and soon thereafter entered into refit in Portsmouth Dockyard and would not return to sea until 26 April 1971. Commander M J A Hornblower took command of the *Leopard* on 10 July 1970. He would have to wait to get the ship to sea though, as her refit and repairs continued until 18 January 1971. Trials and work up's followed throughout the early months of the year. On 26 April, Commander Hornblower finally got his ship underway and steamed out of Portsmouth harbour initially to operate in Home Waters.

On 30 April the frigate arrived at Lisbon in Portugal before taking part in May's *Exercise Rusty Razor*. At the end of the multi-national exercise on 10 May *Leopard* sailed up the River Tamar and secured alongside at Devonport for two days. On 12 May she sailed to pay a courtesy visit to Dover, before continuing across the North Sea on 14 May to visit Antwerp. Two very enjoyable days were spent there before she again sailed this time around the top of Scotland and down through the Western Isles to arrive at the Clyde on 18 May. There, three days were spent conducting intensive training before arriving at Portsmouth on 22 May. After a brief call at Weymouth, *Leopard* assumed the role of Gibraltar Guardship until 1 July. Upon being relieved *Leopard* returned to Portsmouth for a period of maintenance, which lasted until 6 August.

After post maintenance trials in early August, *Leopard* took part in *Exercise Mainhaul* when *Leopard* left Devonport and made her way to Gibraltar, where she arrived on 20 August. The next day saw a two-day visit to Tangiers. The exercise, however, continued until 27 August. *Leopard* stayed in the Mediterranean and went on to visit Izmir, Souda Bay and Corfu before returning to Gibraltar on 24 September, where she entered dry dock on 4 October 1971. The frigate's refit was, however, completed at Portsmouth Dockyard. Where on Valentine's Day 1972, Commander M J Harvey was appointed to command *Leopard*.

Chris Downie recalls his first experiences of *Leopard*, he joined the frigate on 10 April 1972. "She was my first ship and was still in refit in Portsmouth dockyard when I joined her. It was supposed to be a six month refit but due to industrial action by the dockyard staff it took considerably longer. When she came out of refit she had to do the required work up at Portland and we all slogged to complete it. I remember during engine trials the skipper boasting over the ships tannoy that we were now doing 20 knots and before he could stop speaking he had to announce a main machinery breakdown. It was quite a shock for a junior radio operator to join a ship which had equipment that I hadn't been trained on but I was soon taught. It was also quite an experience as I think the Cat Class were the last ships in service to have no dining rooms. You had to make your way from the galley, which was amidships, all the way up forward past the wardroom and into the forward messdeck so you could eat your meals. The forward messdeck was directly below the twin 4.5 inch gun mounting (forward turret). The Cat Class was quite economical ships since they ran on diesel engines. As a result they were ideal for patrol ships. As a result of this we took quite a major part in the cod wars. This was when Iceland decided to increase its fishing limits firstly to 50 miles around its coast and then to 100 miles around its coast. *Leopard* made the national headlines as the ship that had the railway lines sticking out from her sides and stern to act as a determent against the Icelandic gunboats ramming us. Within a few hours of this reaching Whitehall we were ordered to remove them. During the conflict we were asked to shadow the Icelandic Gunboat *Thor,* which we did she led us a merry dance and we eventually ended some where off the coast of Greenland at anchor for the night. The *Thor* rather cheekily signalled us by flashing light and asked us what we thought of the weather up here. Our reply was why don't you accompany us to Portsmouth and we will show you some better weather.

"During this period the *Thor* opened fire to put a shot across the bows of a fishing boat that she was trying to stop fishing. Unfortunately the shot also passed over our bows. We went to action stations and immediately aimed both of our 4.5 inch turrets at her and ordered her not only to stop firing but to put the covers back over her gun immediately she quickly complied. When we were coming off patrol we escorted a fishing trawler back to Hull as she had some sort of engine problems. It was decided that we should escort her right into Hull and spend some time in that City. I remember that no matter what Pub we entered we could not spend our own money as we were classed as local heroes."

After some time spent at Portsmouth on trials, *Leopard* arrived at Devonport on 22 February, but left the next day for the French port of Brest. Three days were spent enjoying the very best of Gaelic hospitality before returning back to Portsmouth and being declared fully operational following the frigate's repairs.

On 3 May *Leopard* sailed from Portsmouth and visited Liverpool for a four-day visit, during which the ship was opened to the public and thousands of Liverpudlians toured the ship throughout the stay in the world famous port. The visit ended when the frigate sailed on 8 May back to Portsmouth. The ongoing political dispute with Iceland over fishery rights in the North Atlantic meant that frigates which had been damaged in collisions at sea with Icelandic gunboats needed to be replaced, and accordingly *Leopard* was sent to the area on 17 June. Her fishery patrol lasted until 5 July.

Following repairs undertaken at Portsmouth, *Leopard* sailed for the warmth of a summer in Gibraltar and ten days spent as guardship for the colony. The continuing pressure to maintain the peace between British trawler men and their Icelandic counterparts meant that Royal Navy escorts were required to maintain a presence at many fishing ports around the coastline of Britain. *Leopard* visited Grimsby on 1 September. Other ports visited in September were Antwerp and Brest, before arriving back at Portsmouth on 17 September.

Two days later on 19 September *Leopard* sailed across the North Sea to the Netherlands and operated with units from the Dutch fleet at Den Helder. Then it was back to the troubled waters around Iceland for another fishery patrol that lasted until 21 October. After three days heading back to the United Kingdom she arrived back at Rosyth, where all necessary repairs to the vessel were undertaken.

November proved to be a busy month when after leaving Rosyth on 5th, *Leopard* arrived at Falmouth before commencing a fishery patrol and some navigation training until 21 November. After a fortnight spent at Rosyth *Leopard* visited Sunderland and Hull in December.

On 20 December *Leopard* arrived at Portsmouth and the crew were rewarded for their work with Christmas leave. On 7 January 1974 the frigate was docked down for maintenance, which was completed on 9 February. Ten days later she slipped out of Portsmouth and headed south to Gibraltar to start her passage to take part in the ongoing Beira Patrol off Mozambique.

March saw port visits to Dakar and Capetown, before the frigate arrived at Simonstown on 22 March. Three days later after restocking her supplies and fuelling *Leopard* started the Beira Patrol, would see the frigate at sea until 4 April. Two days earlier command of the frigate had been transferred to Commander R H Whyte-Melville Jackson. Eight days later *Leopard* was at Mauritius. Later in the month a visit was also paid to Reunion Island before another stint on Beira Patrol that lasted until 7 May. On 16 May *Leopard* arrived at Diego Suarez and this in turn was followed by a visit to the Seychelles.

Leopard then went onto operate in the Persian Gulf, where some of the highlights of the period were the flights from Bandar Abbas to Shiraz, organised by the Imperial Iranian Navy. Two parties of 60 men were flown to Shiraz in aircraft of the Iranian Air Force and taken to see the ruined palace of Persepolis.

The *Leopard* also visited Muscat, Khor Kuwai and Bahrein before sailing across the Arabian Sea to Bombay and then onto Singapore. There as the ship was alongside about twenty wives flew out to Singapore for three weeks. This greatly improved morale amongst some of the crew. *Leopard* spent three days at Surabaya in Indonesia before starting the trip home, with visits to Singapore, Gan, the Seychelles and Simonstown. The frigate arrived back in the United Kingdom in early November 1974.

On 4 November 1974 Lieutenant Commander C A Nix assumed command of the frigate and became the frigate's final commanding officer. Ten days later the ship arrived at Portsmouth and spent the remainder of the year alongside for defects and repairs. Christmas leave was granted to the crew and they returned to the ship in early January 1975.

Between 11 and 25 January 1975 *Leopard* carried out some weapons training at Portland before returning to Portsmouth. In early February *Leopard* was in the Channel area before joining other Royal Navy vessels at Gibraltar for a major exercise.

Sixteen Royal Navy warships and auxiliaries visited Gibraltar over a ten-day period from February 14 1975. The Gibraltar call was after participation in NATO and National exercises in the North Atlantic and before the force moved into the Mediterranean to continue the exercises which lasted until early March. Ships taking part were *Llandaff, Leopard, Ajax, Ashanti, Charybdis, Dido, Fife, Glamorgan, Hermione, Jupiter, Norfolk, Nubian, Onyx, Olympus, Rothesay, Reliant, Black Rover* and *Tidereach*. *Leopard* ventured further into the Mediterranean when on 7 March she reached Grand Harbour at Malta for a five-day visit to the island. She returned to Gibraltar en route to Portsmouth, which was reached on 20 March where more defect repairs were undertaken.

When *Leopard* returned to sea she undertook an intensive period of training around Faslane and the Clyde areas until mid May 1975. On 12 May she arrived at Rosyth before going on to visit Lerwick and HMS *Ganges*. On 3 June *Leopard* returned to Portsmouth.

On 12 June *Leopard* left Portsmouth to visit Ostende and Aberdeen before taken part in a series of exercises before again returning home to Portsmouth on 3 July. Summer leave was granted to the crew before *Leopard* slipped out of port on 18 August and headed for Gibraltar. *Leopard* visited Malta in late August before assuming the role of Gibraltar guardship until 3 October. During her time as guardship, *Leopard* crossed the Straits of Gibraltar and visited Tangier for four days from 11 September. The day after she was replaced as guardship at Gibraltar, *Leopard* sailed to visit the huge French naval base at Toulon, where she arrived after two days steaming.

Leopard arrived back at Gibraltar on 12 October and after two days alongside left for the return passage to Portsmouth. After she had arrived back in the United Kingdom she entered into a dry dock at Portsmouth Dockyard for a further period of defects and repairs, which were completed on 3 November.

Two days later having slipped out of Portsmouth, *Leopard* arrived at Rosyth to undertake a Distant Water Fish Patrol that included a number of port visits to Harstad. On 26 November *Leopard* returned to Rosyth. Two days later she crossed the North Sea for her final foreign port of call to Amsterdam. Six-days were spent in the Dutch port with the crew enjoying the local hospitality and breweries. *Leopard* left Amsterdam on 4 December and arrived at Portsmouth with her paying off pennant flying from the mainmast. The frigate's final voyage, however, started on 11 December when she sailed from Portsmouth to cover the short distance to Chatham Dockyard in Kent.

On 12 December 1975 *Leopard* arrived at Chatham Dockyard at 09.20 in the morning. Later in the day the ceremony to officially de-commission the frigate was completed and the ensign was lowered on *Leopard's* quarterdeck. In the weeks ahead, the frigate was moved to the standby squadron and was mothballed in a state of preservation.

The call to return to service never happened and *Leopard* spent the next two years at Chatham Dockyard awaiting the final journey to the scrapyard. On 6 July 1977 she was finally sold for scrapping to A. Howden & Co and taken from Chatham Dockyard on 12 December 1977 passing through the South Lock of the Dockyard at 10.00.

In order to get the frigate up the creek on the River Thames at Dartford, *Leopard* had to be cut into two pieces and then towed up the creek, where final demolition was to be carried out. Within the space a year nothing remained of *Leopard*.

CHICHESTER

The second member of the Type 61 class was laid down at the yard of Fairfield Shipbuilding and Engineering at Govan on 26 June 1953. Construction proceeded well until 21 April when *Chichester* was launched into the waters of the River Clyde by the Countess of Home, wife of the Right Honourable Earl of Home, PC. Lieutenant Commander H W Drummond was appointed at commanding officer on 23 May 1956. *Chichester's* completion, however, took another three years and by the time she entered Royal Navy service Lieutenant Commander Drummond, had been replaced by Commander R D Butt on 15 April 1958.

Chichester was provisionally accepted on Friday May 16 1958 and the following day the frigate sailed from Glasgow. Her destination was Torbay where she arrived after an overnight sailing. After two days at anchor off the Devon town, *Chichester* set sail for Chatham Dockyard, where she arrived on 21 May. Crowds had gathered along the River Medway to greet the latest design in Royal Navy frigates and many amongst the crowds were somewhat bemused by what they saw, most asked the obvious question, which was, "where is her funnel?"

After a week at Chatham, *Chichester* eased back to sea for the short voyage to Portsmouth, where she pulled into port on 30 May. A whole month was spent alongside before she ventured to sea again on 28 June when she sailed for Portland, arriving on the same day.

June 1958 gave way to July and a weeklong visit to Milford Haven was laid on. On 2 August she left port and sailed up the Irish Sea to take part in exercises in the Moray Firth with other units of the Royal Navy. Scottish waters were left behind as the frigate sailed south and crossed the English Channel to take in the delights of a short official visit to the French port of Cherbourg from 8 August. Two days later she sailed for exercises and returned to Chatham Dockyard after three days at sea.

On 3 September *Chichester* left Portsmouth and headed for Milford Haven again. There she would take part in a dramatic rescue of the Costa Rican steamer *Concha,* which had caught fire off the Pembrokeshire coast. *Chichester* had been taking part in an exercise with the Radar Direction School, HMS *Harrier*, not far away when news reached the frigate of the dangerous situation.

The fire onboard the merchant ship was so intense that *Chichester's* boarding party could not take their hoses and fire fighting equipment near enough to the seat of the fire and after an explosion which shook the ship and increased her list by some three feet the party withdrew.

Shortly afterwards tugs arrived from Pembroke and took the burning ship under tow but she sank before reaching port. Following the drama the frigate sailed from Milford Haven on 17 September for the overnight passage to Devonport. Another four days were spent in port before *Chichester* returned to sea. By 26 September she had arrived at Gibraltar and then onto the Mediterranean with the aircraft carrier *Albion*. The ships then sailed for the Far East. After a twenty-four hour stop over in Malta, *Albion* together with the cruiser *Sheffield* and the frigate *Chichester*, left for Port Said, which was reached on Friday 31 October.

On Wednesday 5 November the ships finally arrived at Aden to find the colony in the throes of a general strike, stirred up by Egyptian President Nasser's agents in the Yemen. Despite the unrest five days were spent there before sailing on 10 November with the aircraft carrier *Albion* or Karachi. The remainder of November was spent at sea operating in the Indian Ocean with *Albion. Chichester* arrived at Singapore on 29 November with *Albion* and the destroyer *Cavalier*. The Royal Navy force remained in port until mid December when they sailed for Hong Kong, arriving at the Colony on 19 December and spent Christmas there. One of the first visits of the New Year occurred on 29 January 1959 when *Chichester* visited Port Blair in the Andaman Islands, where fresh water was taken onboard.

On the first day of February *Chichester* was at Calcutta in India with the cruiser *Ceylon*. Whilst later in the month she arrived at Hong Kong on 21 February as an escort to the Royal Yacht *Britannia*. The Royal Yacht with the Duke of Edinburgh onboard and

Admiral Sir Gerald V Gladstone, KCB, Commander-in Chief of the Far East Station joined other ships including *Ceylon, Queensborough, Quiberon, Cheviot* and *Cavalier*.

After a very enjoyable visit to the colony the force slipped to sea and headed south. On 26 February the crew of *Chichester* prepared themselves and the ship for the crossing the line ceremony. King Neptune was welcomed onboard and those found guilty of some 'serious' crimes were dunked in the traditional ceremony.

Next landfall for the frigate occurred on 5 March when she arrived at Albany in Western Australia, where the crew got some fresh milk for their tea. When she put into port at Fremantle the crew left the ship for a period and many enjoyed the long sandy golden beaches. This was followed by a period in the Great Australian Bite with the cruiser *HMNZS Royalist*.

Next came a six day voyage across the Great Australian Bite during which planned flying exercises were cancelled owing to adverse weather conditions, but the *Albion* rejoined *Chichester*, which had steamed down from Calcutta, and the destroyers *Voyager* and *Cheviot*, together with the *RFA Resurgent*. All five ships then set course for Fremantle, where they arrived on Saturday 14 March for a four-day visit.

With the Australian cruise at an end, *Albion* and the other four ships steamed north, bound once again for Singapore. During the passage, they were joined by *HMAS Melbourne* and the cruiser's *Royalist* and *Ceylon*. Apart from the exercises carried out by this sizeable fleet, the only real excitement came during the passage through the Sunda Strait when two Indonesian MIG-17's flew low overhead.

The submarine *Andrew* surfaced and requested medical help from *Chichester*. One of the submarines' crew was unwell and *Chichester's* doctor was transferred to the submarine. On 25 April the frigate arrived in the Philippines at Manila before sailing back to Singapore and started work for her participation in the large *Operation 'Showboat'*, which concluded on 2 June when *Chichester* arrived at Nossi Be. After three days she slipped and again headed in a southerly direction for Simonstown, where she arrived after five days steaming.

The next twenty days were spent in port conducting self- maintenance and granting leave. When she left on 30 June *Chichester's* course took her across the Atlantic, where her first port of call was on 13 July at Mar De Plata. Two more visits were planned before the frigate started her journey north across the Equator and into the waters of the River Tamar. The first of these visits was to Rosario on 20 July and after that the fantastically vibrant and flamboyant city that is Rio de Janeiro in Brazil. At both locations the crew were greeted by local dignitaries and made to feel most welcome.

On 3 August *Chichester* left the delights of Rio de Janeiro behind as she headed northwards and finally arrived at Plymouth on 17 August. She refuelled and returned to sea after only a few hours in port. The next day after steaming up the English Channel, *Chichester* entered the Thames Estuary and arrived at Chatham where she entered into refit. On 17 September 1959 *Chichester's* crew welcomed onboard her latest commanding officer, in the shape of Commander D W Foster. The refit was completed on 5 February 1960 and she conducted sea trials that concluded at Portland in mid March 1960. She returned to Chatham Dockyard to take part in that year's Chatham Navy days held over the weekend that started on 16 April. The next three days saw hundreds of people looking over the frigate and asking the crew on duty all manner of questions about the weapons, electronics and crew accommodation.

Further trials were carried out at Portland through until 20 May when she left for Gibraltar and a deployment to the Mediterranean. In the coming months, *Chichester* went onto visit Malta, Alicante, Cannes, Cyprus and Bari before returning to Malta on 22 August for a period of self-maintenance. The next stage of her Mediterranean cruise took in visits to Bone, Cartagena and some exercises before paying a four-day visit to Palma, where some of the crew enjoyed runs ashore. From Palma it was a short trip to Gibraltar and thence back to Chatham Dockyard, which was reached on 31 October. *Chichester* was taken in hand at the Dockyard for a refit that would last until Easter the following year.

On 21 April 1961 *Chichester* left Chatham for Portsmouth, where she stayed for the remainder of the month. On the first day of May *Chichester* sailed into the Solent and thence onto Portland areas for trials, which would last until 21 June. The crew had been expecting to visit the United States, but this cruise was cancelled because of the crisis in

Kuwait, which was being threatened by the larger and more aggressive neighbour Iraq. On 22 June she arrived back at Portsmouth and eight days later sailed with *Rhyl* and the aircraft carrier *Hermes* to the Mediterranean instead of the planned American cruise.

On 4 July *Chichester, Rhyl* and *Hermes* arrived at Gibraltar. After some exercises in the Mediterranean with other Royal Navy units, there was another week at Gibraltar, before leaving again on four more day's exercises. The Middle East, meanwhile, had calmed noticeably and the requirement for support had abated somewhat. *Chichester* and the other ships were recalled back to the UK.

On 15 August *Chichester* arrived at Chatham before travelling onto Portsmouth. With the prospect of a stateside trip gone, the crew of the frigate must have wondered what lay in store for them. Eventually when the ship left Portsmouth on 20 August they discovered that the schedule had a voyage to the Far East planned. She crossed the Mediterranean with a stop at Malta, before arriving at Port Said on 27 August. The frigate travelled through the Suez Canal and also saw her transfer to the Far East Station. The next day she left the Suez Canal and continued her journey to Aden.

Three days were spent alongside, refuelling and replenishing supplies before she sailed to the Persian Gulf to begin a patrol in the area that only a few months before had been at such a risk of conflict and she also visited Kuwait. The patrol was completed without incident and on 8 October *Chichester* arrived at Mombassa for a maintenance period, which concluded on 22 October.

Eight days later she was back in the Persian Gulf and commenced another patrol of the troubled waters, until sailing for Singapore at the beginning of November. There she acted as a plane guard for the aircraft carrier *Victorious*, returning to Singapore on 18 November.

Another period of maintenance was carried out before the ship carried out some exercises in local waters with friendly nations. 1962 started well for the frigate with more exercises and in late January a visit to the beautiful island of Trincomalee with its equally beautiful large natural harbour in which the frigate anchored. The visit was relatively brief, *Chichester* leaving on 2 February for Bahrain, via Gan. She arrived at Bahrain on 13

February and was amazed by the welcome the ship received at the port from the locals, who wanted to explore the ship and meet the crew. The ongoing conflict in Indonesia, however, required the frigate's presence and on 21 February she left for dhow patrol. After an uneventful few days on the patrol, *Chichester* retraced her course and returned to Bahrain, but not before conducting the exercise *A WEX 5* en-route.

After eight-days in Bahrain *Chichester* slipped from the quayside on 12 March. Next ports of call were at Abu Dhabi and Aden before a return to Singapore on 28 March for more exercises, which also took her to the Subic Bay area where she operated with the US Navy

After the exercises were completed, *Chichester* sailed for Hong Kong, where she arrived on 17 May. Some amongst the hundred plus crew of the frigate had never been to the colony and for them it was a huge learning experience. Nine days were spent in Hong Kong before the ship sailed for Okinawa and a tour of Japan.

The planned schedule saw visits to the city ports of Yokosuka and Komatsushima. If the welcome in the Gulf States had overwhelmed the crew of the frigate, the reception in Japan was staggering. At each of the ports the ship was besieged by thousands of well wisher's. The crew, once away from their ship were allowed time to explore the cities and to learn about Japanese culture. On 12 June *Chichester* sailed from the harbour at Komatsushima and returned to the American military base on Okinawa; after which Singapore was reached on 30 June.

After some maintenance the ship left on 16 July and started her journey back home to the United Kingdom via Gan, the Suez Canal and Malta. On 7 August she arrived at Gibraltar and stayed for two days. *Chichester* was to take part in mid August's *Exercise Riptide* and during the exercise the frigate exercised with no less than three aircraft carrier's *Hermes*, and the massive US aircraft carriers *Forrestal* and *Enterprise*. On 15 August the exercise finished and *Chichester* slipped away from the other ships and continued her voyage back to Chatham where she arrived three days later. She remained at Chatham until 21 September.

Autumn 1962 saw a visit to Southend and in early October, participation in *Exercise Sharp Squall* until 18 October. On the same day she arrived at Devonport, where she remained until taking part in *No 9 NATO JSC* until 22 November and this was followed by *JASCENT*. On 4 December *Chichester* arrived at Leith for a six-day visit, before returning to Chatham Dockyard. Christmas leave was granted and on 7 January 1963 *Chichester* was taken in hand for another long refit.

She remained in dockyard hands throughout the whole of 1963 and into the summer of the following year. During the refit, the most obvious alteration in the frigate's appearance was the plating over of her mainmast, which had previously been of a lattice construction. *Chichester* re-commissioned on June 17 1964 at Chatham under the command of Commander G A Rowan-Thomson who had assumed command on 6 April 1964.

After working up at Portland throughout the summer and early autumn, *Chichester* took part in October's *Exercise Hallmark 13* and November's *Exercise Limejug* held in the waters around Londonderry. On 3 December the frigate sailed for the return journey to Chatham, where she arrived after two days steaming around Britain's coastline.

On the penultimate day of 1964, *Chichester* was docked down within Chatham Dockyard for a maintenance period, which was completed on 11 January when the frigate slipped out of Basin 3 and into the River Medway. The maintenance period had fully prepared *Chichester* for the rigours of an extended deployment to the Far East. Her first destination on this journey was Gibraltar, where she arrived after four days at sea. After stops at Malta and the passage through the Suez Canal, *Chichester* arrived at Aden on 2 February for a two-day stopover.

She crossed the hot and tropical conditions in the Indian Ocean and first landfall was the small island of Gan where the ship's stores were restocked and her fuel tanks were replenished. Before long *Chichester* resumed her voyage to Singapore, where she arrived on 15 February.

March was spent at Singapore or involved in the Indonesian Confrontation but the opportunity was also taken to continue training during Flag Officers Training *Exercise*

FOTEX which was undertaken in the Andaman Sea and in the Strait of Malaca. Later twelve days were spent on banyans on Pulau Langkawi. On 27 March *Chichester* and all the other ships involved in the exercises returned to Singapore to prepare for *Exercise Showpiece*, which included the Australian aircraft carrier *Melbourne* and the American 'carrier *Bennington*. The Royal Navy force included the frigate's *Chichester, Plymouth* and the destroyer *Agincourt*. The exercise finished in the Gulf of Thailand on Saturday 22 May and *Chichester* paid a visit to the vibrant and exciting city of Bangkok. This was followed by a return on 26 May to Singapore.

After a brief maintenance period, *Chichester* returned to sea on 11 June for *exercise Windy Weather* in the Sarawak area. After eight gruelling days at sea the frigate returned to Singapore, where she remained until sailing for plane guard duties to *Ark Royal* until 17 July. On the same day *Chichester* entered the port at Penang to a wonderful welcome from the locals. Only three days were spent in this bustling port and much of the time of the officers was spent conducting VIP's around the ship or carrying out civic functions and visits. *Chichester* arrived back at Singapore on 21 July.

Three days later she arrived at Hong Kong for a six day's stay before sailing with the frigate *Plymouth* for Singapore. This was the start of *Chichester's* journey home to the United Kingdom and together with the *Plymouth*, she visited Gan, Aden, the Suez Canal and Malta during August. On 3 September the two warships arrived at Gibraltar and spent three days at the Rock before continuing the journey to Plymouth but on 10 September *Chichester* was finally home at Chatham Dockyard.

The following month on 15 October she completed a docking and essential defects period after which she sailed to Portland, where except for a visit to Portsmouth she stayed for almost the entire month. On 28 October *Chichester* arrived at Gibraltar for a brief visit before leaving in company with the frigate *Plymouth* and the destroyer *Cambrian* for the waters off Londonderry. The remainder of the month was spent conducting crew training before crossing the North Sea and paying a courtesy visit to the port of Rotterdam on 25 November. After a very enjoyable visit that also included a visit to a local brewery amongst many organised runs ashore, the ship slipped out of the massive port on 1 December and set a course for Portsmouth, where the following morning she arrived with the destroyer *Cambrian*. Soon after she returned to Chatham where she docked in preparation for *Chichester's* next deployment East of Suez set for early in the New Year. Christmas and New Year leave was granted to the crew and they were told to prepare to be away from home for at least six to nine months upon their return to the ship. On 7 January 1966 the essential maintenance was completed and four days later *Chichester* left Chatham Dockyard in the company of the frigate *Plymouth*. The pair would travel to the Far East together and called at Gibraltar, Malta and Suez before calling at Aden on 28 January and Gan on 2 February. Finally the two frigates arrived on time at Singapore on 7 February. Between 14 and 22 February *Chichester* took part in *Exercise MillStream* before returning to Singapore on the last day of the exercise. After a period of maintenance at Singapore *Chichester* sailed from the Naval Base and conducted a series of exercises that culminated on 17 May when she left the island of Tawau for *Exercise Sea Imp*. This exercise involved warships from Britain, USA, Australia, New Zealand and the Philippines. After initial harbour and sea training exercises, the main part of the program involved convoy operations that ended in the Gulf of Thailand on June 9. On the way to Hong Kong *Chichester* gave assistance to the American cargo ship *SS C R Musser*. A crewmember had been injured onboard and *Chichester* launched her seaboat to transfer the man to the frigate for a fast transit to Hong Kong.

The summer was spent shuttling between Singapore, where she conducted numerous periods of self-maintenance at Hong Kong before arriving on 8 September at Seria where the ship was wined and dined by officials from the Shell Company. After two days the frigate slipped and returned once more to Singapore for a short refit, which was finished on 17 December 1966.

After trials at Singapore she left the naval base on 8 February 1967 and sailed to Hong Kong principally to take part in *FOTEX* until 18 March before returning to Singapore. When she next ventured to sea on 19 April she visited Christmas Island and the Australian city of Fremantle before crossing the Indian Ocean to operate with the aircraft carrier *Victorious* on the Beira patrol in the Mozambique Channel. The area would become very familiar to the crew of *Chichester* and her sister ships' as their long endurance proved ideal for staying in the patrol areas for extended periods. Except for a brief four-day visit to

Mombassa *Chichester* remained on station until 1 August. Two days later the crew were pleased to see the welcoming sights and sounds of Simonstown. After five days ashore the warship slipped on the start of her return journey to the United Kingdom. After a fuelling stop at Freetown, *Chichester* arrived at Gibraltar on 25 August, where she stayed overnight before continuing the crossing of the English Channel to Portsmouth. After a night *Chichester* sailed for and arrived at Chatham on 31 August and almost immediately entered into refit.

On 19 September 1967 command of the frigate was transferred to Commander T D Kitson, who had previously been assigned to the Royal Navy's Tactical School at Woolwich. *Chichester* was re-commissioned at Chatham Dockyard on October 7 1967. Amongst the guests at the ceremony were Vice Admiral John Parker, Captain Douglas Charles Woolf and Captain D V Morgan. The ships commissioning cake was cut by Mrs Kitson and Junior Seaman Graham Johnson.

Chichester left Chatham Dockyard on Monday 23 October to start a lengthy series of trials throughout the next few months. Christmas leave was granted to the crew and only on 30 January 1968 did she leave Portsmouth bound for Portland, where she arrived the same day. She was exercising there with *Argonaut, Danae, Ulster* and *RFA Engadine* when Admiral Sir John Bush, Commander in Chief, Western Fleet and Rear Admiral J C Y Roxburgh visited the ship.

In early February *Chichester* left Portland and headed north to Rosyth, where she would become involved in the role of fishery protection duties. She visited Tromso, Harstad and Hammerfest in Norway, during what became known as Norway Fishery Patrol, before arriving back at Portsmouth on 8 March. The frigate remained in port until 21 March when she sailed for a courtesy visit to the town of Sunderland. Three enjoyable days were spent in the Northeast industrial town before crossing the North Sea for an equally impressive visit to Rotterdam. She returned to Chatham Dockyard for a maintenance period, which saw her remain in dockyard hands until 6 May.

Upon her return to the fleet, *Chichester's* first port of call was to Londonderry, where she arrived on 20 May before retracing her route to Portsmouth in the beginning of

June. She carried out some training at Portland before arriving off Ipswich for an official visit to the boys training establishment at HMS *Ganges* on 15 June. The next day another cross channel trip to Antwerp for a four-day visit. On 22 June *Chichester* started a month long period of shuttling between Portland and Portsmouth.

In July *Chichester* was in the Clyde and Scottish areas, with visits paid to Rothesay, Faslane and participation in the large scale *Exercise FORTHEX*, which finished on 3 August. Indeed, it was during July that the ship caused something of a political row between Russia and Britain. The Russian's claimed that *Chichester* was spying on Russian naval exercises being held off North Norway together with the Russian ships being buzzed by NATO aircraft. *Chichester* was in fact on fishery patrol duties at the time. On 9 August the frigate crossed the Irish Sea to visit Belfast for a few days.

On Friday 23 August *Chichester* arrived at Chatham Dockyard principally to take part in Chatham Navy Days. Many hundreds of local residents from the Medway Town's poured into the Navy Base and toured the ships on display over the two-day event held on Sunday 1 and Monday 2 September. After her public appearance the frigate entered into an interim refit that occupied the remainder of the year.

On 4 November 1968 Commander T J F Sex took command of *Chichester*. It was to be sometime, however, before he took the ship to sea. *Chichester* re-commissioned at Chatham on May 23 1969. The ships commissioning cake was cut by junior seaman Ashley Stockley and the Captain's wife.

A "Well done" message was passed by Admiral Superintendent, Vice Admiral Sir John Parker, to all concerned in the refit of *Chichester*. On leaving Chatham Dockyard the ship sent the following signal in reply:

"Thank you very much for my refit and for the help and consideration given to my ship. Dockyard men at all levels have combined to give us a great start to our commission. Please pass them my thanks."

After visits to Portsmouth and Portland in June the frigate was at Portsmouth on 16 July when she was declared operational and continued her shakedown throughout the remainder of July. She arrived at Portsmouth on 15 August. Ten days later the ship paid a courtesy call to the city of Hull, during which local VIP's were greeted on board the frigate and toured the ship. *Chichester* left Hull after four days and after a period at sea returned to Chatham on 12 September.

Chichester's next deployment would again take her to the Beira Patrol. She left Chatham Dockyard on 20 October and after calling at Portsmouth and Portland for weapons training and crew training sailed south via Gibraltar and arrived at Simonstown on 18 November 1969. Dave Clarke who served on *Chichester* at the time, recalls that during the stay, "the crew made the nightly trip on the old rickety train down for a run ashore in Capetown, visiting Daryls, the Navigator's Den to name just a couple of the bars and clubs. About 4.30 in the morning, we all jumped back on the train for the long journey back to Simonstown, always worse for wear." After the brief stay at the port *Chichester* slipped on 23 November.

Three days later she started work on the Beira patrol, where she spent the next month sailing up and down intercepting any ships suspected of oil smuggling. On 30 December she was relieved on duty and the frigate returned to Mombassa where she spent a somewhat belated New Year's celebrations on 5 January 1970. Soon after the ship slipped and sailed north. The port of Masirch was reached on 10 January, for a two-day visit before sailing on to a scheduled arrival at Bahrain on 14 January.

The oil rich country was most welcoming to the British frigate and those crewmember's granted shore leave were greeted by friendly and hospitable locals who wished the crew well. Later in the month *Chichester* arrived at Massawa on 31 January for the Ethiopian Navy Days with the CNFG Commodore K Lee White, embarked.

Whilst in Massawa the opportunity was taken to challenge the visiting ships, including a Russian destroyer, to various sporting activities. In swimming, water polo, track and field sports *Chichester* had the best record of all visiting ships and second only to the Ethiopian Navy.

When the *Chichester* received the Emperor Haile Selassie with a Royal Salute, he met officers and ratings and was entertained to tea and crumpets with strawberry jam, a traditional gesture from the Royal Navy to the Emperor. *Chichester's* visit was, however, marred by the sudden and tragic death of Commander Timothy J F Sex her Commanding Officer at the time. The Commander suffered a brain haemorrhage, whilst onboard *Chichester* and was rushed to hospital, but did not survive.

Chichester sailed on 5 February 1970 with the Executive Officer in charge and then onto the Gulf. Later in the month *Chichester* crossed the Indian Ocean and arrived at Hong Kong, where some exercises with other Royal Navy units were planned but were cancelled due to poor weather. On 28 February 1970 command was transferred to Commander N H N Wright. During her time in the Far East *Chichester* undertook a wide variety of tasks that included giving assistance to the Shell oil tanker *Mactra* after an explosion onboard. The frigate also took part in the major Far East re-enforcement exercise *Bersatu Padu*. This exercise involved over fifty ships, two hundred aircraft and 20,000 men from Australia, New Zealand, Malaya, Singapore and the United Kingdom.

In March 1970, *Chichester* visited Chabar Bahar, Jask, Bandar Abbas, Qishm, Lingeh, Charak and on 10 March Kharg Island in Iran. At Kharg Island she stayed overnight sailing the following day for Bandar Shapar. On 15 March *Chichester* made a return visit to Bahrain. Some repairs were necessary to the warship and local facilities at Bahrain were used to carry these out, with the repairs being completed on 24 March.

Three days were spent in Kuwait, with another spell in Bahrain bringing March 1970 to a close. On leaving port the commanding officer decided he did not need the assistance of the local tugs and as a result hit a large sandbank, which almost crippled both of the frigate's propellers. As David Clarke recounts, it was a dramatic moment. "At the time of hitting the sandbank, myself and another RO33, Nigel Lohman, were down the radio operator's mess painting the deckheads. Our mess was directly over the propellers, and when the stern of the ship started bucking like a bucking bronco, we didn't need to be told twice to evacuate what was a potentially very dangerous situation. This led to a change of the ship's programme and off we limped towards Singapore. *Chichester's* duties were handed over to *Andromeda*, who had their six-week tour of Australia cancelled. *Andromeda's* crew were not at all happy and therefore it came as no surprise when *Andromeda's* helicopter on one occasion flour bombed *Chichester*, scoring a number of hits on the giant double bedstead Type 965P radar set. On 7 April *Chichester* arrived at

Colombo for further repairs before making for Singapore for a more substantial refit, which saw the ship once again in dockyard hands until 7 May.

Three days later *Chichester* sailed for the Subic area to exercise with US Navy units before arriving at Hong Kong on 16 May. At the colony she took part in *Exercise Crackshot* until 5 June, when she arrived at Singapore. Soon after another major naval exercise, *Exercise Matlock* took place until 25 June, which saw the frigate within three days steaming of Hong Kong. She arrived at HMS *Tamar* on 28 June. On 9 July *Chichester* sailed for Singapore for another maintenance period that would prepare the ship for the long voyage home to the United Kingdom. *Chichester* left Singapore on 4 August for Australia with visits to Fremantle and Geraldton before calling at the exotic location of Mauritius, where many of the crewmembers enjoyed the very briefest of visits because within hours *Chichester* had resumed her journey to Bahrain.

The following month *Chichester* represented Britain at the Ethiopian Navy Days on her way home, after which she travelled through the Suez Canal and visiting Malta before arriving at Gibraltar on 2 October. Three days at Gibraltar allowed the crew time buy presents for friends and families and to take part in the traditional top of the rock race. *Chichester* slipped from her berth on 5 October and arrived at Portsmouth on 8 October for a short visit. On 13 October *Chichester* sailed up the River Medway and was soon secured within Chatham Dockyard for a refit.

The refit was completed on 9 November and after a visit to Portsmouth, *Chichester* operated with the aircraft carrier *Eagle* until 6 December. The next day saw her taking part in the three-day *Exercise Centigrade*. Two days later she arrived at Hull before returning to Chatham Dockyard on 17 December for Christmas leave.

1971 started for *Chichester* when she slipped out of Chatham Dockyard and into the River Medway. Within the hour she was in the Thames Estuary and turned right into the English Channel and raced around the coastline to arrive in the Clyde two days later. She operated in the Clyde and Faslane areas until arriving at the Port of Glasgow on 23 January. She was open to the public on some of the four days she spent in port and the crew greeted many hundreds who toured the frigate. On 29 January *Chichester* arrived back at Chatham dockyard for another maintenance period, which was completed towards the end of February.

On 26 February she arrived at Portsmouth having left Chatham four days earlier. After some navigational training *Chichester* visited Grimsby on 4 March and started another stint on fishery patrol duties in the North Sea and the waters off Norway. During this period *Chichester* would visit Tromso twice, before taking part in *JMC 161* between 22 and 26 March, when she arrived at Rosyth.

After three days in port, the frigate sailed again to protect the fishermen at North Cape. The conditions at North Cape were very cold and with choppy seas, but after three days in the area *Chichester's* crew drew a deep sigh of relief when they were told to return to Rosyth. The ship spent almost a week at the Scottish Navy Base before sailing south for Chatham, where she arrived on 17 April.

At Chatham Dockyard the opportunity was taken to refit and recondition the frigate over the next seven weeks. Lieutenant Commander E (WE) A A Crump was appointed as the frigates temporary commanding officer during the course of her refit. *Chichester* was at Chatham Dockyard when together with the frigate *Lowestoft* she played host to a force of German ships when they called at Chatham Dockyard. The Federal German Navy force comprised the destroyer *Z3* and the corvettes *Triton, Najade, Theseus* and the oiler *Eifel*.

Chichester sailed from Chatham on 21 May and headed south to Gibraltar to assume guard-ship duties until 10 June when the frigate sailed for Palermo. A very enjoyable visit was had by all and many fond memories were captured on film when the warship sailed for Malta on 16 June. Grand Harbour on the Mediterranean Island was a welcoming sight for the crew of *Chichester* after three days at sea. Sadly, it was only to be a short visit because the frigate slipped out of port on 20 June and started the six-day voyage to Alghero. It was soon time to retrace the course back to Gibraltar, via a five day stop at Palma. There was only time to refuel and restore at Gibraltar before *Chichester* headed back to sea and a return to the United Kingdom. On 12 July the frigate entered the Solent and was soon entering Portsmouth harbour to secure alongside.

After three days *Chichester* again sailed and headed up the North Sea to arrive at Rosyth on 17 July. Her final foreign visit was on August 11 which saw the start of a five-day visit to the town of Haugesund before starting the return trip to Rosyth. Rosyth would become the frigate's new home for the next few months as the frigate was stripped of a large proportion of her equipment to prepare her for a brand new role as guard-ship at Hong Kong. As part of the refit the ship's Type 965 radar was removed, but its mast was retained. As a consequence of the reduction in top weight extra two 40mm guns were mounted.

On 5 June 1972 Commander E H M Orme assumed command. By early summer the refit was completed and after trials at Portland, the frigate arrived on 22 September at Portsmouth and declared operational. Late September and October was spent at Portland carrying out work up's before a visit to Frederikshaven on 17 November. After five days in port the ship sailed back across the North Sea to Rosyth. After two days in the dockyard *Chichester* slipped out on 26 November to take part in *JMC 166* until 8 December. The final preparations for *Chichester's* departure to Hong Kong were undertaken in mid January, before she left Portsmouth on 23 January. Her route to the Far East took the frigate to Gibraltar and Bathurst, where she arrived on 1 February.

Chichester was welcomed by the locals and European community on arrival at Bathurst in Gambia. The ship's crew took part in a sports programme with the highlight being a shooting contest against the Gambian Defence Force, which *Chichester* won decisively.

Next stop for the frigate was a six-day stop over at Simonstown, before she started a Beira patrol. The boredom of the patrol was alleviated by a port visit to Mauritius on 3 March. On 2 April *Chichester* arrived at Gan, which was followed the next day by a call at the island of Male. She stayed there for two days before sailing for a planned arrival at Colombo. Sporting fixtures were organised against teams from the Sri Lankan defence forces. The opportunity was taken to allow onboard staff from the Sri Lankan Navy for midshipman training. Having returned the men after their two-days at sea with the Royal Navy, *Chichester* left on 13 April left and sailed in company with the Australian ships *HMAS Perth* and *HMAS Derwent* for two days of exercises before going onto Singapore.

Only three days were spent in port before *Chichester* sailed once more, this time to finally arrive at her base of operations for the foreseeable future, Hong Kong.

As she arrived in port she was welcomed by a large number of local boats and junks together with the resident Royal Navy vessels at the colony. Having been at sea for a lengthy period *Chichester* was dry-docked until 9 May undergoing essential maintenance, but upon her re-emergence she immediately started to work up as Hong Kong guardship.

Chichester left Hong Kong on 26 June to visit Bangkok as part of the ANZUK forces in the area, to which *Chichester* was assigned until 15 July 1973. During this period the frigate also visited Subic Bay.

One of her duties in Hong Kong was the interception of illegal smuggling, particularly of drugs and in July, *Chichester* was involved in the capture of a large quantity of drugs. AB Martin 'Buster' Brown of *Chichester* had found the sacks at a depth of 100 feet, held down by about 280 pound weights and secured in a- fishing net. Five Royal Navy divers recovered three out of six sacks, which had been reported dumped overboard from a local junk. The sacks were later taken to the offices of the Narcotics Board where their value was estimated at £66,000.

The next month *Chichester* sailed from Hong Kong on 23 August to participate in *Exercise Green Light*, which lasted until 31 August. Upon her return to Hong Kong the frigate was alongside at HMS Tamar for a couple of weeks before visiting Japan. Port visits were laid on there to Kagoshima, Sasebo and Hakata throughout September and early October. On 5 October *Chichester* arrived at the Japanese Island of Okinawa, where she remained until returning to Hong Kong.

The following month, *Chichester* was taken into a dock for another period of maintenance, which was completed on Christmas Eve. After a break for the festive season the ship started her trials in the New Year, which were concluded on 14 January. Subic Bay area was her first 'foreign' port of call in 1974 and throughout February, *Chichester* started shuttling between Subic and Hong Kong that lasted until 9 March when the frigate arrived at Singapore. There, *Chichester* was again assigned to the ANZUK force and as such took part in *PASSEX* between 19 and 21 March.

The exercise finished with the assembled ships sailing into Singapore on the last day. After a couple of days *Chichester* slipped from alongside and visited the Philippines capital of Manila. Further exercises were conducted in the Subic Bay area until she sailed for Hong Kong on 4 April.

On 21 May 1974 Lieutenant Commander D E Ranger took command the frigate. Commander R P Warwick later replaced him in command. *Chichester* continued to operate in Hong Kong waters throughout the summer and autumn of 1974. On 11 November she left Hong Kong to take up her duties as the Royal Navy's contribution to the ANZUK force. She carried out these duties until 5 December, which included visits to Bagkok, Singapore and Medan before arriving back at Hong Kong on 7 December.

Christmas and the Western New Year was spent at the colony and it was 17 February 1975 before *Chichester* left Hong Kong again to exercise in the Subic areas. Towards the end of the month along with the frigate *Mermaid*, *Chichester* took part in *Exercise Sea Fox*. At the end of the exercise *Chichester* went onto visit Manila between 11 and 13 March. Two days later she was back at Hong Kong for essential repairs, which included a docking period until 19 April.

On 15 May she visited Pusan in Korea and Maizuru and Niigata in Japan. After leaving the latter on 3 June *Chichester* steamed for six days to return to Hong Kong. In June 1975 and just before being host to the Queen and Duke of Edinburgh at Hong Kong, *Chichester* was involved in one of the greatest sea rescues of all time.

The Danish vessel *Clara Maersk*, had picked up 4,620 refugees from Vietnam and sent out an emergency call for medical aid. The *Chichester* was despatched with all speed to the area and after storing left port within two hours of receiving the emergency call. She carried with her fully equipped medical teams and medicines, blankets, food and water. Upon reaching the ship medical teams assessed the condition of the refugees and provided all necessary care before the *Clara Maersk* carried them to safety.

Upon her return to Hong Kong *Chichester* had the pleasure to play host to the Queen and Duke of Edinburgh and watched a firework display – the first such event since 1967 when fireworks were banned in the colony.

On 4 July 1975 *Chichester's* executive officer Lieutenant Commander G R Scanes took temporary command of the frigate whilst Commander Warwick left the ship for a few months. September 1975 proved to be a very busy month for *Chichester* with visits to Singapore, Penang, Bangkok and Subic Bay areas to operate with other navies and to show the flag before arriving back at Hong Kong on 13 November.

1976 saw a continuation of the usual routine in the colony with numerous port visits and exercises with friendly nations in the area. 1976 was, however, also the year designated as *Chichester's* last on station as Hong Kong Guardship and preparations were made for the frigate's withdrawal. During the course of the next few months a great many locals, who had played a part in making *Chichester's* tour of duty such a success were welcomed onboard. These people ranged from local politicians to local artists and laundry workers.

One of the last of many goodwill visits occurred on 14 May when *Chichester* visited Pitcairn Island from 11.00 am to 09.00 hours on 17 May. The ship had transported Mr H Smedley, Governor of Pitcairn, Henderson, Ducie and Oeno Islands to and from the island in the course of an official visit. There was 'a right royal feast' at the conclusion of the visit with much of the food prepared by *Chichester's* crew supplemented by local food and drink.

In June *Chichester's* time as Hong Kong guardship came to an end and after an emotional farewell to the colony that had been her home for four years, she sailed back to the United Kingdom. *Chichester's* course home would take in twelve ports of call and take 20,000 miles via Cape Town to Portsmouth.

Her first port of call after leaving the Colony on March 31 was Manila. Then it was onto Guam, followed by visits to the Solomon Islands, Fiji, the Falkland Islands, Montevideo, Recile, the Cape Verde islands and Gibraltar. Finally on 23 July 1976 *Chichester* sailed up the River Medway and arrived at Chatham Dockyard, where she was decommissioned and placed into reserve.

After two years she was placed on the disposal list in 1978. She remained safely within the protective walls of the dockyard until she was sold for scrap. Her masts and engines were removed and sold to the Malaysian Navy and by June 1980 most of the frigate's equipment had been removed. On St Patrick's Day 1981 tugs arrived to manoeuvre the redundant frigate from her lay up berth in No 2 Basin, through the much larger No 3 Basin and into the Bullnose that led to the River Medway. Stripped of all useful equipment including her masts and engines, *Chichester* looked somewhat bare as she was eased out of Chatham Dockyard for the very last time. The dockyard tugs handed over to sea going vessels just outside of the Bullnose and these tugs started the long tow to Queenborough in Scotland where demolition of the once proud frigate commenced almost upon her arrival.

LYNX

Built by John Brown shipbuilders in Glasgow being laid down on August 13 1953 *Lynx* was launched on January 12 1955 by Mary, Princess Royal, Sister of King George VI. The frigates construction continued without any incident and was handed over to the Royal Navy on 14 March 1957. Builders trials were carried out in the Clyde approaches and were found most satisfactory. They were conducted at speeds of 23.41 knots and below over the Arran measured distance between 11 and 18 August 1956. The weather on these trials was reported to be moderate to poor. Full power trials took place at Arran on 25 January 1957 after the trailing edges of the propeller blades had been modified to suppress singing.

Following acceptance of the ship from the shipbuilders *Lynx* travelled south to Portsmouth, where the Royal Navy started their own series of trials. On Friday 19 July 1957, HRH the Princess Royal travelled to Portsmouth and spent a day at sea. She was met by the Commander in Chief Admiral Sir Guy Grantham and the Lord Mayor of Portsmouth and was taken to Admiralty House. As the Royal Party left to drive to South Railway Jetty where *Lynx* was berthed, a Royal salute was fired by the Naval saluting battery in HMS *Dolphin* and all the ships in tidal berth in harbour.

Lynx's Captain J.M.D Gray, OBE, RN was introduced to the Princess. Captain Gray passed through the Royal Naval College and Dartmouth in 1931. He served as a midshipman in the battleship *Nelson* and the cruiser *Enterprise* before serving for a period in the cruiser *Devonshire* during the Spanish Civil War. 1938 saw him specialise as a gunnery officer and as such he joined *Hermes* where he stayed until 1942. His new ship was the anti aircraft cruiser *Spartan* before joining the *Orion* and the battleship *Duke of York*. The post war period also saw Captain Gray serve in the cruisers *Glasgow* and *Swiftsure*. His captaincy was announced in 1955 and he joined the *Lynx* in 1957.

Having successfully passed all the Royal Navy acceptance trials *Lynx* sailed for the South African and South American station on 6 August 1957. The route chosen was to take the frigate to South America first, with visits to Buenos Aires, Montevideo and Rio de

Janeiro in September. The first day of October saw *Lynx* anchor off the isolated British colony of St Helena for two days before continuing her journey to Simonstown.

After a period of self-maintenance *Lynx* left port to visit Capetown, which was reached on 4 December in company with the frigate *Burghead Bay*. The pair of warships left port on 9 December and travelled the short distance back to Simonstown within the day.

The frigate next ventured out to sea on 17 February when she left Simonstown together with *Bigbury Bay* and *Burghead Bay* to visit East London for four-days. On 28 February *Lynx* arrived at Beira, whilst March saw ports of call paid to Durban and Port Elizabeth before returning to Simonstown on 26 March.

Lynx remained alongside until 11 April when she slipped to pay courtesy calls to St Helena and Ascension Island before turning around and heading for Dakar, which was reached on 24 April. *Lynx's* route home to the United Kingdom had been chosen carefully and two days were spent at Dakar carrying out official engagements before resuming the journey back home on 26 April.

On 2 May 1958 she arrived at Portsmouth, where she entered refit, which was completed in mid August. A few weeks previously on 1 August Captain W G Meeke MBE DSC assumed command of *Lynx*. Towards the end of the refit, the crew, were informed that *Lynx* would become a Rosyth based ship on re-commissioning on 16 September 1958. She then headed for Portland, where she would spend the next month working up before returning to Portsmouth.

Lynx left Portsmouth on 18 November 1958 and sailed for the South African and South Atlantic station. She arrived at Simonstown on 20 December to commence her deployment on station. Christmas and New Year were spent in port, before the frigate sailed to Walvis Bay, where she arrived on 7 January 1959. After two days she slipped and in the next few days paid visits to Luderitz and the wide open anchorage of Saldanha before returning to Simonstown on 19 January.

Two days were spent in port before sailing to Capetown for a six-day visit. When she left on 27 January, her course took her into the South Atlantic and the frigate paid visits to Tristan du Cunha and Gough Island, where medical teams checked on the health of the scientists who had made Gough Island their temporary home.

Lynx returned to Simonstown on 7 February. Later in February she returned to Saldanha for a ten-day stay that lasted until 20 February, with the frigates arrival back at Simonstown. March would see visits to Luanda, Lobito and Mossamedes before arriving back at Simonstown on 25 March. *Lynx* was taken in hand by the dockyard for a docking and for repairs to be carried out. This lasted until 11 May when she left Simonstown.

Lynx sailed into the Indian Ocean and visited Lourenco Marques after five days at sea. Four days were spent there before sailing onto Mauritius, which was reached on 25 May. Next port of call was reached on 3 June when *Lynx* arrived at Majunga. On 6 June she slipped to sea once more and headed back towards South Africa and a planned arrival at Durban on 10 June. Six days of hectic sporting and social engagements followed for the crew after which *Lynx* returned to Simonstown.

The South American leg of her deployment started on 30 June and made for the other side of the South Atlantic Ocean. On 14 July, the frigate arrived in Argentina's Capital City of Buenos Aires for a five-day official visit. The port that was established to service the beef exporting business, after which the product was named was next on the list, Fray Bentos proved to be a very interesting port of call for all the crew. *Lynx* sailed on 23 July and started her return journey to South Africa, which also saw stops at the British dependencies at Ascension Island and St Helena. On 21 August *Lynx* sailed into port at Simonstown.

Seasonal leave was granted as *Lynx* herself received maintenance within Simonstown Dockyard throughout September. On 6 October 1959 *Lynx* sailed from Simonstown, for a planned visit to Port Elizabeth and onward journey back to the United Kingdom. After stops at Durban and Freetown, on 11 November *Lynx* arrived at Gibraltar and left the following morning. Finally after nearly two years away the frigate returned to Portsmouth on 16 November and was soon taken in hand by dockyard workers for a refit. The next four months were spent at Portsmouth, as staff in the dockyard repaired and corrected all the defects found and replaced numerous pieces of equipment onboard that were worn out or obsolete. The refit was completed on 25 March 1960.

Prior to her refit completion, 9 February 1960 saw the appointment of Captain R A Begg to command the frigate *Lynx*. Later in April the frigate was finally returned to operational status and following a series of trials and work up's throughout late spring and early summer 1960, *Lynx* sailed from the United Kingdom on August 3 1960. She then visited Lisbon, Tenerife, Freetown, Vitoria, Rio de Janeiro, Ascension Island, Port Harcourt, Luana, Saldahna, Simonstown, Cape Town and Lourenco Marques. October and November 1960 was taken up with *CAPEX* exercises. In late November, *Lynx* visited Capetown before returning to Simonstown on 5 December, where she spent Christmas and New Year carrying out a period of self-maintenance until 17 January 1961. Two hundred people who had helped the ship during this period alongside were thanked by being given a cruise from Simonstown to Cape Town.

The following day she left Simonstown for Port Elizabeth and Lourenco-Marques, where she arrived on 26 January. After four days there she continued her journey around the coast of South Africa with a visit to Durban. February would be just as busy with frequent calls to Simonstown and amongst the interesting ports of call were Mauritius, Takoradi, Nacula and Diego Suarez. *Lynx* also took part in exercises with the aircraft carrier *Victorious* in mid February. On 24 April 1961 *Lynx* arrived at Freetown to represent the United Kingdom at Sierra Leone's Independence Day. Once the many and varied events staged to celebrate the day had been completed, *Lynx* sailed on 30 April for Dakar, where she arrived three days later. After a brief stop over at Port Etienne, *Lynx* started the passage across the Atlantic to commence the Caribbean leg of the deployment.

On 14 May *Lynx* arrived at Trinidad and went onto to visit San Juan, Culebra and Bermuda by the end of May. After a successful bombardment of an unfortunate West Indian island *Lynx* sailed to Bermuda for ten days self maintenance and the Queen's birthday parade. The maintenance was done at Ireland Island and it rained almost everyday. For the last weekend of the visit the ship moved to Hamilton. The weather behaved, as it should in Bermuda and the Queen's birthday Parade was conducted in brilliant sunshine. The frigate sailed to the southern states of the United States in mid June, with visits to Charleston and Jacksonville, before resuming her patrols in the Caribbean with a one night stay at Caysal Bank on 21 June. The delights of Kingston, Jamaica welcomed the frigate and crew three days later.

July 1961 continued in a similar fashion with visits, at la Guaira, port for Caracus as guests of the Venezuelan government.

The ships' visit co-incided with the 150th anniversary of Venezuela's independence. Field Marshall Lord Alexander of Tunis, *Lynx* and the band of the 1st Battalion the Royal Hampshire Regiment represented Britain. *Lynx's* guard, were allowed to march through the city with bayonets fixed past President Betancourt in the Avenue of National Heroes.

After a visit to Port of Spain, *Lynx* sailed into Bridgetown on the island of Barbados for a four-day stay. Much of this time was spent preparing the ship for the North Atlantic passage back to Britain where she arrived on 4 August at 11.10 in the morning. About 250 relatives and friends went out to Spithead by tug to join the ship and returned in her to the dockyard. The next three days were Portsmouth Navy Days and *Lynx* was opened to the public.

After some leave *Lynx* left Portsmouth on 9 September for an appointment at Copenhagen via the Kiel Canal. Copenhagen was reached on 11 September 1961. It was only an overnight stay before the frigate again slipped away to sea to take part in the three-day *Exercise Freshwater* in local waters that lasted until 15 September. Following the successful completion of this exercise, *Lynx* paid a four-day visit to Ronne, before resuming training off the coast of Londonderry throughout September. On 14 October *Lynx* left for *Exercise Sharp Squall* until 27 October, which ended with the frigate's arrival at Rosyth.

Politics between Iceland and Britain had hit a low in 1961 over fishery rights and a number of Royal Navy warships were despatched to the rough waters around Iceland to protect British interests, *Lynx* was amongst these vessels. She left on her first patrol on 18 November from Rosyth. The patrol started two days later and lasted until 5 December 1961.

After spending Christmas at Portsmouth, *Lynx* paid a brief visit to Ponta Delgada on 2 February and returned to Portsmouth three days later. *Lynx* arrived at Chatham Dockyard and paid off on 8 February before entering into an extensive refit. The refit, however, was undertaken at Portsmouth Dockyard, the frigate having been towed to the Hampshire yard. The refit would take over two years to complete and saw the ship virtually rebuilt with many new additions made to the ships equipment and her armaments were updated. Crew accommodation was also enhanced.

On 5 May 1963 command of *Lynx* was transferred to Captain P M Austin and the next day the frigate returned to Chatham Dockyard. Captain Austin had joined the Royal Navy in the 1930's and in the course of his wartime career served in the cruiser *Cornwall* and in numerous destroyers. Postwar he chose to purse a career as a naval aviator and having gained his wings, served in 807 and 736 squadrons in aircraft carriers such as *HMAS Sydney* during the conflict in Korea. He also served in the *Bulwark* and *Eagle* before taking command of *Lynx*. Minor modifications were carried out on the frigate as the work up continued in the English Channel and Thames Estuary. On 30 May 1963 *Lynx* was re-commissioned at Chatham as Leader of the 7th Frigate Squadron. The frigate, however, continued to work up throughout the summer months of 1963 and returned to Chatham Dockyard on frequent occasions.

On 2 September *Lynx* began her work up at Portland, where she remained until 17 October before arriving at Portsmouth. Having been declared operational to the fleet, *Lynx* quickly began to take on operational duties including working with the submarine commanding officers course in the Clyde estuary, where the frigate was both target and hunter for the submarine commanders to combat. This was followed, by more training in the Londonderry areas, until a return to Portsmouth on 6 December.

On 8 December the frigate was docked in order to prepare the ship for her extended deployment to the South Africa and South American Station. On Friday 10 January friends and families of the crew were guests onboard *Lynx*. Three days later she sailed from Portsmouth and started her journey to her base of operations at Simonstown. The frigate visited Gibraltar and on 24 January arrived at Sao Vicente on the Cape Verde Islands; this was followed, by a refuelling stop at Freetown on 29 January. The last day of

January saw *Lynx* arrive at Takoradi, whilst the following month was a very busy one for the frigate with visits to Monrovia, Freetown, Douala and on 19 February Santa Isabel. *Lynx* finally arrived at Simonstown on 27 February.

At Simonstown the frigate wore the flag of Vice Admiral Sir Fitzroy Talbot, C in C South Atlantic and South America station. Later in Easter 1964 saw *Lynx* at Simonstown, when two ratings from *Lynx* were spending their Easter leave climbing on Table Mountain. On the Saturday night the two men, PO.Elect Donald London and EA Dennis Blake- camped on a ledge above a ravine leading to Devils Peak. At about two in the morning they were awakened by a heavy fall of rock into the ravine, followed by moaning and shouts for help.

On investigation, they found that a team of four Cape Town University students had been attempting to scale the ravine with no lights and ropes. One of who fell fifty feet and sustained a broken rib, which punctured a lung. London and Blake carried out a textbook rescue of the injured people.

The Admiralty had been preparing a major Royal Navy deployment for a number of years, and they had determined that an area that had not seen a large naval force for some time was South America. Accordingly, their Lordship's designed a task force centred on the cruiser *Tiger*, the County class destroyer *London*, and frigates *Penelope, Lynx*, the submarine *Odin* and *RFA Wave Chief*. These ships would visit a number of South American ports and extend the hand of friendship and also use the opportunity to sell military hardware to those countries.

Lynx joined the force and on Sunday 20 September arrived with the submarine *Odin* at Admiralty Bay, Bequia. Two days later Vice Admiral Sir Fitzroy Talbot transferred his flag from *Lynx* to the cruiser *Tiger*. Next port of call was to La Guaira, port for Caracus where no less than 12,000 people visited the four ships in port. Such was the success of the visit that many people had to be turned away from touring the ships.

On Thursday 1 October it was the turn of Cartagena and five days later on Tuesday 6 October *Lynx* arrived at Panama with *Tiger, Penelope, Odin* and *Wave Chief.*

She sailed through the canal and headed into the Atlantic. First port of call on this leg was on 10 October at Guayaquil for a three-day port visit.

The Royal Navy ships continued their tour of South American ports with *Lynx* visiting Talcahuano and Punta Arenas with *Tiger, London, Penelope, Odin* and *Wave Chief*. These ships slipped to sea on 6 November and made the relatively short voyage to Montevideo, where they arrived on 11 November. Having left Uruguay on 16 November, *Lynx* sailed south to arrive at Buenos Aires together with the other ships of the force the next day.

Six days were spent in the Argentine Capital City and the sales force onboard the cruiser and escorts, achieved substantial military sales to the Argentineans. The Argentinean Navy would eventually place orders for two Type 42 destroyers, then in the early stages of development. Further sales occurred in Brazil, where two Oberon class submarines were ordered. *Lynx* and the other Royal Navy warships arrived at Rio de Janeiro on 27 November and stayed until 2 December.

Having completed the South American leg of the tour, *Tiger, Lynx, Penelope* and *Odin* headed out into the Atlantic and exercised together en-route to Dakar, which was reached on 9 December. *Lynx* returned to Devonport on 16 December, but only stayed overnight before completing her journey to Portsmouth the next day with the cruiser *Tiger*.

Captain P G R Mitchell MVO assumed command on 4 January 1965. Repairs were completed on the frigate by 22 January 1965. Three days later *Lynx* arrived at Portland and stayed in the area until 3 February when she slipped and made her way to Londonderry. The body of Admiral Sir Denis Boyd, who died at Portsmouth on January 21st, was buried at sea from *Lynx* on January 27. A naval helicopter flew overhead and dropped a wreath into the sea during the ceremony.

Four days were spent at Belfast from 11 February before arriving on 19 February in the Clyde area for S/M A.1 that lasted until 27 February. The second part of the course S/M A.2 also required her presence and *Lynx* remained in the area until returning to Portsmouth on 6 March 1965. A fortnight later *Lynx* conducted some trials before visiting

Aalborg from 29 March until 2 April 1965. The following few days were spent undertaking FOS/MC.

Lynx entered into refit at Portsmouth during the late spring of 1965 that would keep her out of service until October. Following work up's in the English Channel and at Portland, *Lynx* was declared operational to the fleet on 17 January 1966 following repairs at Portsmouth. The next day she arrived at Portland, where she would stay until 9 March when she sailed back to Portsmouth.

Lynx's planned program for the next few months, must have delighted many amongst her crew, as the frigate was detailed to sail to the Caribbean and assume the Bahamian Patrol. Unlike the Beira patrol, the numerous islands in the area provided a wealth of interesting places to visit for the crew. On 28 March she sailed from Portsmouth and visited Ponta Delgada, before starting the Atlantic crossing to Bermuda, which was reached on 7 April. Seven days later *Lynx* started the Bahamian patrol. During May 1966 the frigate visited Chaguaramas, Tobago and on 24 May arrived at British Guiana for the independence celebrations. The crew took part in the official ceremony as representatives of the British government. After-two days *Lynx* sailed for Barbados. After two days at sea, she arrived at the island's capital for a short stay.

On 2 June 1966 *Lynx* left and arrived at Grenada the same day for another all too brief visit for many amongst the frigate's crew. The following morning, *Lynx* returned to sea to visit Martinque. June would also see ports of call paid to San Juan and Bermuda on 14 July. After four-days in port, *Lynx* started the return journey to Portsmouth, where she arrived on 29 July.

On 1 August *Lynx* entered a dry-dock for repairs and a short refit. The frigate's latest commanding officer, Captain J G Jungius assumed command of the frigate on 2 August. Jungius joined the Royal Navy as a cadet at the Royal Naval College at Dartmouth in 1937. He served as a midshipman in the battleship *Rodney* and the cruiser *London*. In 1943 Jungius joined the 59th Landing Craft Assault Flotilla and took part in the Allied Landings in Sicily. He was promoted to the rank of Commander in 1955 and Captain in June 1963 and served as an Assistant Director in the Naval Tactical and Weapons Policy

Division of the Ministry of Defence until 1966. The rest of August, however, saw the frigate firmly staying put within the confines of Portsmouth Dockyard and only on the last day of the month, was *Lynx* floating once more.

Most of September was spent at Portland, working up the ship and crew. On 22 September *Lynx* was at Portland for *Exercise LINK WEST* that lasted until 2 October. She returned to Portsmouth the next day and remained there until 12 October when she sailed for Bremen. The German City welcomed the warship for four days that started on 13 October. Having left *Lynx* crossed the North Sea and returned to Portland for a few days before securing alongside at Portsmouth on 21 October for some repairs to be undertaken.

Lynx left Portsmouth on 28 November and sailed south, where she escorted the aircraft carrier *Hermes* to Gibraltar. Both ships arrived at Gibraltar on 2 December for a short overnight stay. The next morning *Lynx* continued her journey south to join the South African and South American Station. After a four-day visit to Tema, which ended on 16 December, *Lynx* continued onto Simonstown, which was reached two days before Christmas. The festive season was celebrated onboard and amongst many of the shore establishments at Simonstown with some good-natured sailors who may have one too many drinks.

1967 started well for *Lynx* when she slipped out of Simonstown on 11 January bound for the Mozambique Channel, where she would stay until 3 February. Four days later she arrived back at Simonstown for a docking period. Another fortnight in the Mozambique Channel enforcing United Nations sanctions against Rhodesia followed before arriving on St Patrick's Day at East London, where the Irish members of the crew 'celebrated' their patron saint in suitable style.

Lynx sailed on 22 March for Port Elizabeth, where she arrived the next day. For the next six days the ship's company were entertained by the local residents and challenged to a variety of sporting and social events. This certainly made up for the boredom experienced on the Beira Patrol, where the ship would sail up and down the line looking out for merchant ships, which might be trying to break the blockade. Another great port visit was had at Durban from 30 March before resuming the Beira Patrol until 17 April.

On 11 April 1967 *Lynx* had been transferred to the command of C in C Home Fleet following the Royal Navy's withdrawal from South African waters. She had been the last ship to be based at Simonstown. On 21 April 1967 *Lynx* arrived at Simonstown for a short docking period. This was followed by a six-day courtesy call to Durban, before again returning to Simonstown.

After a fortnight alongside, *Lynx* slipped to sea on 17 June together with the destroyer *Kent* and the frigate *Arethusa* for exercises with the South African Navy which were completed the next day. On 22 June the frigate arrived at the desolate and lonely outpost of the British Empire, the island of Tristan da Cunha

The mid-winter weather conditions made communications with the islanders difficult but some flew to the ships in the squadron's helicopters from *Kent* and *Arethusa*.

A most unusual event occurred soon after, when *Lynx* received a distress call from the liner *Darwin*. A heavily pregnant Mrs Beggs from South Georgia was onboard the liner *Darwin* when it was discovered that her baby was due two months prematurely, the help of *Lynx* was sought in taking her to Port Stanley and the medical facilities there.

The baby christened Pauline arrived shortly after *Lynx* arrived at Port Stanley on June 27 1967. Mother and child spent the night onboard and were taken ashore the next day, the baby in a special weatherproof cradle made by shipwright Douglas Lesanto.

The remainder of *Lynx's* South American deployment was just as eventful with the first of a large number of port visits taking place on 6 July when she called in at Buenos Aires. This was followed soon after for exercises with the Argentine navy in the River Plate area that lasted until 18 July when the frigate arrived at Rio de Janeiro. The visit to Rio de Janeiro saw the world famous beaches frequented by a large number of British sailors. After a brief visit to Salvador, *Lynx* spent August in the Caribbean when she called on Georgetown, San Juan and spent time on the Bahamas Patrol until 29 August. *Lynx's* next port of call was on 2 September when she arrived at Bermuda. The frigate remained in port for twenty days allowing the crew to enjoy the island and its many natural treasures. On

22 September *Lynx* sailed north to visit the United States Naval Academy at Annapolis, where she arrived on 25 September. This visit, was followed by another to Newport in the state of Rhode Island

Lynx returned to the Caribbean on 9 October, when she visited the US facilities at Guantanamo Bay. The next day she resumed the Bahamian patrol, which finally finished on 5 November. Before starting her return passage across the North Atlantic to Britain, *Lynx* visited Freeport and Bermuda, before leaving the latter port on 13 November.

On 23 November 1967 *Lynx* returned to Devonport and soon commenced a much-needed refit. Four days later saw a change of command, when Captain J G Junggius left the ship and handed over command to Commander G J F Slocock. The frigate's refit would take almost all of 1968 to be completed.

On 11 October 1968 the Royal Navy was hoping to have a real live *Lynx* at the commissioning of *Lynx*. A local zoo was contacted but said it would be too risky, as these animals are not 'really friendly enough'. In the end, a stuffed Lynx was provided for the event. On the day of commissioning, heavy rain put pay to the planned quayside ceremony and as a result the event was moved to the drill shed at HMS *Drake*. Despite the elements being unpredictable, the 220 ratings and 15 officers of the frigate paraded before senior officers, family and friends. Commander Geoffrey Slocock read the commissioning warrant and his wife then cut the commissioning cake decorated with a Lynx.

Lynx sailed to pay a goodwill visit to Ostende from 16 to 20 October before returning to Portland the next day. Portland would become very familiar to the crew of the frigate because she was to remain there until 11 December. The next day *Lynx* was back within the confines of Devonport. Having left the dockyard on 16 December, *Lynx* sailed north to Faslane.

On 18 December *Lynx* was in the Clyde exercise areas, where she remained for the next three days. The crew had been informed that leave would be granted to them upon their return to Devonport, where she arrived two days before Christmas. *Lynx* remained in port throughout the festive season and only ventured to sea on 20 January 1969 for the short passage to Portland. *Lynx* went onto operate off Culdrose with helicopters and aircraft from the Royal Naval Air Station throughout 21/22 January, before sailing onto Londonderry.

On 9 February *Lynx* arrived back at Devonport for a five-day self-maintenance period. After this, *Lynx* went onto operate in the Clyde exercises areas and around Faslane with the submarine commanding officer training courses, before crossing the North Sea for an official visit to the German port of Bremen on 4 March. Four days later she slipped to visit Wilshelmshaven, before returning to Devonport on 10 March.

The remainder of the month was spent alongside before slipping to sea on 31 March. Her course took her to the Mediterranean via Gibraltar. At Malta on 10 April *Lynx's* crew were employed carrying out a short period of self-maintenance, before taking part in April's *SUBEX* exercise.

April and May, saw the frigate remaining in the general area of Malta, and took part in a series of naval exercises, including *Exercise Dawn Patrol*, which finished with a port visit to Naples between 1 and 6 May 1969. On 19 May *Lynx* arrived back at Gibraltar and took over the role of Gibraltar guardship. On 6 June she too was replaced and sailed for Devonport, where she arrived after three days at sea.

Lynx's planned program had been planned many months before and it had been decided that the ship would sail to the Far East in summer 1969. To prepare the frigate, she was taken in hand for a docking period on 16 June. On 22 July 1969 Commander B Prideaux took command of the frigate. Three days later *Lynx's* repairs had been completed and the crew started to work up the ship.

On 1 August *Lynx* finally left Devonport and sailed south down the coast of Africa, with stops at Gibraltar and Freetown before arriving at Simonstown on 21 August. Seven days later *Lynx* slipped from port and started her stint on Beira patrol on the first day of September. The remainder of the month was spent on patrol. The boredom of the patrol was broken by occasional interceptions of merchant vessels. On 2 October *Lynx* arrived at the island of Farquhar. October would also see visits to Gan, Singapore and Hong Kong, where she arrived on 18 October.

The frigate stayed in the colony until 10 November, plenty of time for old matelots to re-acquaint themselves with the best local facilities, whilst newer crewmembers on their first visits to Hong Kong were introduced to the delights for the first time. *Lynx* left on 10 November and headed towards the Philippines and Australia. After visiting Subic for an overnight stay on 12-13 November, *Lynx* sailed onto Townsville and Mackay, being the largest Royal Navy warship seen at the sugar port since the Second World War. On 25 November she arrived at Sydney, where self-maintenance was carried out. *Lynx* spent thirteen days at Sydney and there were a large number of official and social obligations to be undertaken. There were also a number of opportunities to take things a little less seriously. A small number of men left the ship at Sydney for a 'walk about' cross-country to Port Lincoln and Adelaide – some 750 miles distant.

Four days later she paid a port of call to Port Lincoln for a three-day visit. The festive season was spent at Adelaide, where *Lynx* had arrived on 18 December and the only ill effect of the visit were scratches to the Captain's arms when being photographed with Lynx kittens in Adelaide zoo. On 27 December she sailed to visit Albany, where the crew took part in numerous New Year celebrations. The next day *Lynx* slipped out of port and resumed her planned itinerary that saw her go onto visit Manila, Bangkok and Penang. *Lynx* arrived at Singapore on 9 January 1970 for maintenance of essential equipment. Some shore leave was also granted to the crew before the frigate slipped on 19 January to take part in *JANEX*.

At the end of the exercise *Lynx* returned to Singapore for further maintenance. The end of the month saw *Lynx* visit Farquhar and Gan. She slipped out of port on 5 March with *Galatea* to sail to Hong Kong, where she arrived on 9 March. Almost all of the month was spent at the colony, with frequent and colourful trips into the city for the crew. When she did return to sea, *Lynx* left on 21 March and set a course for Manila to take part in *PX41*.

Early April 1970 saw ports of call paid to Sattahip, Bangkok, Singapore and on 24 April *Lynx* sailed for the overnight passage to Penang. Four days later she left and arrived back at Singapore the same day.

The frigate started her refit on 8 May when she was docked down. The refit continued until 20 July when she re-commissioned at Singapore Naval Base and became the last Royal Navy warship to re-commission at the base. Mrs Empson, wife of the Commander Far East Fleet, Vice Admiral L D Empson cut the commissioning cake assisted by J S Tom Farthing the youngest member of *Lynx's* crew.

The summer months were spent working up in the waters off Singapore; *Lynx* finally left Singapore on 17 September and after five-days steaming arrived at Hong Kong. After a period of self-maintenance *Lynx* sailed to Geraldton in Australia, where she arrived on 5 November. Three days later *Lynx* participated in *Exercise Swan Lake* that finished when the frigate sailed into Fremantle.

Eight days later on 23 November command of the frigate was transferred to Commander A J White. He took her to the Singapore areas towards the end of the month, before turning around and heading for Okinawa, where she arrived on 2 December. Ten-days were spent on the island before sailing back to Singapore for Christmas and New Year.

On 11 January 1971 *Lynx* slipped from port en route for home. She made a fuel stop at the island of Gan and another three days later on 19 January at Farquhar. The route chosen around the Cape of Good Hope would allow the frigate to be used in the ongoing Beira Patrol and *Lynx* dutifully assumed this role on 22 January. A month of intercepting and where practicable boarding and inspecting vessels suspected of carrying oil for Rhodesia started. Sailors onboard all the Royal Navy vessels were frequently bored by the monotony of this operation. Days would go by without any shipping and in the meantime *Lynx* would sail up and down a designated line continually monitoring and being on the lookout for potential blockade-runners.

When she was relieved on station on 22 February, the crew happily received the news that a week was to be spent at Simonstown from 26 February. The city's bars and taverns were said to be full of sailors relieved to be away from the boredom of the Beira patrol. On 5 March *Lynx* sailed from Simonstown to sail up the West Coast of Africa. She made no stops until arriving at Gibraltar on 19 March for three-days alongside the Mole.

On 25 March *Lynx* arrived at Devonport, where she entered refit on 12 April 1971 after de-storing had been completed.

Lynx spent the rest of 1971 in refit at Devonport, with most of her compartments being refurbished and modernised. Her engines and electronics were overhauled and where necessary replaced with newer more efficient units. The gun barrels of the twin turrets were also exchanged with new one's with fresh linings. Finally the refit was completed on the last day of 1971. The first few months of 1972 were spent shuttling between Portland and Devonport during the frigate's work-up's.

When *Lynx* left Devonport on 15 March 1972 she started a period of her career in home waters. On 29 March she was declared operational to the fleet, however, her shakedown continued until early April. After a spell at Portland and Devonport, *Lynx* sailed north to visit the Scottish fishing port of Oban for four-days from 17 June before sailing across the North Sea. *Lynx* arrived at Kristiansand in Sweden for a five-day visit to the city on 31 June. On the return journey to the United Kingdom, the opportunity was taken for some weapons training in the North Sea before arriving at Portsmouth on 30 June.

July proved to be a very busy month starting with a six-day visit to the Welsh port of Llandudno and participation in a large- scale naval exercise, which started on 17 July. *Lynx* and sister-ship *Jaguar* both took part in *Exercise West Hoe* off Plymouth, together with *Fife, Blake, Achilles, Caprice* and *Bulwark*. At the end of the exercise *Lynx* returned to Devonport dockyard. July also saw the frigate sail north to operate on the Clyde before returning south to arrive at Portsmouth on 31 July. *Lynx* entered into dry dock for an extended maintenance period to prepare the frigate for a lengthy period at sea. The maintenance was completed on 29 August.

Following ports of call to Devonport and Portland *Lynx* sailed on 8 September for Madera. Her next port of call was to Freetown, where *Lynx* arrived on 18 September. After two days the ship was back at sea and on 25 September Commander C H Layman took command of *Lynx*. Three days later *Lynx* arrived in the familiar surroundings of

Simonstown. She remained there until 5 October when she sailed for the Mozambique Channel.

It was whilst in the Mozambique Channel an act of supreme bravery was noted in the ship's log. On 21 October Petty Officer W J Hudson dived into wild, shark- infested seas off Mozambique and cut free an officer who was trapped in a capsized life raft. The incident occurred after *Lynx* had sped to the scene when the Taiwan ship *TUNG KING* foundered on a coral reef pounded by huge waves. In an 11-hour non-stop battle with the sea, all 22 people on board were saved. A whaler from *Lynx* picked up 9 survivors before starting a hazardous operation to rescue the 13 left on the ship.

Those people were taken off through mountainous surf and encircling sharks. The first lieutenant of *Lynx*, Lieutenant Commander G D Hotehkiss led the rescue and it was during the rescue that he became entangled and was rescued. As a line was put aboard the wreck the seas mounted and the rescue task was made more difficult because many of the survivors could not swim. After being examined by the MD the survivors were transferred to the Greek merchant ship *Hellenic Destiny*.

The following month *Lynx* went to the aid of an ill seaman on a Kenyan freighter. The seaman, by the name of Salim Bukhet had a perforated appendix and was transferred from the freighter to the frigate for a speedy transit to Ilma de Mozambique, where the unfortunate sailor was flown to the nearest hospital facilities.

In December 1972 *Lynx* visited the island of Labuan off Sabah, whilst later during a visit to Belawan in Northern Sumatra links were forged with the Indonesian Naval Forces. *Lynx* took part in an impromptu exercise called *'Exercise Friendship'* when *Lynx* operated with a squadron of Russian built Riga class frigates.

Having made valuable friends during the frigate's time in the Far East, 1973 started with a period of time spent at Hong Kong, where she arrived on 19 January. Friendly rivalry between *Lynx* and *HMNZS Otago* came to a head at Hong Kong with a relay race between Tamar and the Peak, the steep hill overlooking Victoria Harbour. Three teams competed in the gruelling run; the *Lynx* 'A' team winning in 27 minutes 46.6 seconds.

Before starting her voyage home to Devonport *Lynx* spent a spell as Hong Kong guardship. There the crew was asked to build a playground near a school in a fishing village. In mid February 1973 whilst at Singapore, *Lynx* was assigned to the ANZUK force. With a visit on 19 February 1973 *Lynx* arrived at Medan for a four-day visit, before retracing her route back to Singapore for a period of weapons training. The homeward journey to Britain continued throughout March when the frigate visited Muscat and Khnor Kuwai. This was followed by visits to Dubai and Bahrein, where the British frigate carried out a series of exercises with the local naval forces.

On 12 May *Lynx* arrived at Bandar Abbas. Whilst entering Bandur Shahpur *Lynx* received a distress call from a Somali vessel called *Sun Po* that said she had lost two men overboard. The *Lynx* altered course to assist and lowered her whaler. The men were found in the water and taken back to their ship. Later whilst at Bandur Shahpur for three days many sporting fixtures were held with the Iranian Armed forces and the local chemical's company.

In mid May the frigate visited Masirah followed by Mombassa from the 23 May. After four days the frigate slipped to sea and arrived at Simonstown on 4 June. Six days later after many social and sporting activities had been undertaken with good results for *Lynx*, she left port to take part in *SANEX* until the following day. On 22 June she arrived at Dakar for a short two-day stop before resuming her long passage to Devonport, where she entered dry dock.

On 25 June the frigate's latest commanding officer joined the ship, he was Lieutenant Commander N St J Morley-Hall. One of the first VIP's to visit the frigate during his time in command visited the ship on 3 July. Liberal MP for Rochdale, Mr Cyril Smith MP toured the ship together with thirty of his constituents and his mother. The dockyard work on the frigate was completed on 9 July.

Lynx put to sea for three-days in August for weapons training before sailing north to Rosyth, where she arrived on 11 August. The frigate was required to undertake a fishery patrol in the waters around Iceland. The dispute between Iceland and Britain had reached a new low and the Royal Navy had been asked to provide a large number of escorts to protect the British trawlers conducting their business in the region. *Lynx* started her extended patrol on 14 August.

Much has been written about the tactics of the Icelandic gunboats but much less about how the British trawler-men thanked the Royal Navy for their protection. One trawler skipper asked if *Lynx's* Captain had a preference for a particular kind of fish. Told that he rather fancied a small turbut for dinner the trawler skipper sent over the smallest he had, - a turbut four feet long! *Lynx's* patrol came to an end on 10 September when she headed back to Devonport.

After spending seven days at Devonport, she left the dockyard to arrive at Dover on 21 September. During her stay at Dover the crew were reminded of the previous HMS Lynx the shore base at Dover that operated throughout the Second World War and which was bombed on several occasions with a large loss of life. On 28 September *Lynx* was back at Devonport, where seasonal leave was granted to the crew. The frigate next ventured to sea on 22 October when she left Devonport to carry out weapons training before visiting Gibraltar on 30 October. *Lynx* remained in the general area of Gibraltar until mid December acting as the colony's guardship. She arrived back at Devonport in time for Christmas leave to be granted on 21 December 1973.

1974 started with some weapons training in the English Channel towards the end of January. After a period of maintenance, *Lynx* carried out more weapons training off Portland until sailing north for Rosyth, where she arrived on 22 February. After three days she sailed to take part in *JMC 741*, which was, followed by navigational training, in mid March. On 16 March the frigate arrived at Devonport. *Lynx* remained alongside taking on extra supplies of promotional material for the public at the start of a Meet the Navy visit to Workington. During her visit one third of the town's population visited the ship during the visit. On day one the crew counted 1,672 visitors, the next the figure shot up to over 5,000.

On 3 April the frigate was back at Devonport and after a spell alongside *Lynx* left for the Mediterranean. She arrived at Gibraltar on 25 April and carried out duties associated with being the colony's guardship for almost a month. She arrived at Malta on

10 May for a four-day stay before continuing her voyage in the Mediterranean. Her first stop was at Keflanlini before going onto visit Zakinthos and the Greek Capital of Athens on 4 June. *Lynx* tied up alongside at Piraeus for the visit, which lasted just one day. She was one of a number of warships that had assembled at Piraeus for *Exercise Dale Falcon*, which concluded on 15 June. Two days later the frigate was back at Malta. After a visit to Gibraltar en route to home waters *Lynx* sailed up the English Channel and into the North Sea to arrive at Rosyth, where she arrived on 27 June. *Lynx*, was joined by the frigate's', *Apollo* and *Plymouth* as the three ships entered port in line ahead, with *Lynx* at the rear of the column. It was perhaps fitting that *Lynx* was the last ship in the column as it had been decided that the frigate would have a brief refit at Rosyth to prepare the vessel for the Standby Squadron at Chatham Dockyard. As she arrived at Chatham she flew her paying off pennant which fluttered across the River Medway, all 340 feet of it!

Derek Henderson recalls his association with *Lynx*. "With regards to my time on *HMS Lynx*, I only served on her for approx eight weeks as a fill in draft whilst waiting to join a NATO draft. I was on her from February 76. The vessel at this time was in the process of having equipment removed prior to being mothballed. I spent most of my time doing fire watch for the dockyard mateys or bilge water level checks. The only memorable incident I can recall was when the dockyard welder I was doing fire watch for said it was time to break for lunch. I informed him that I had to stay for at least 15 minutes to ensure nothing caught fire from smouldering bits of metal. He said "dinnae worry laddie nithins (nothing) gan tae catch fire here so awa fur yer dinner". So off I jolly well went and you can imagine the consternation I felt on arriving back at the vessel to find two fire tenders there and you guessed it, the fire had been in the department that I was supposed to have checked. I was hauled up in front of the duty DO but the dockyard matey had already told everyone we had stayed for the regulatory time so it could not be helped and I just went along with the story. Needless to say from then until the time I left I always stayed for at least half an hour after any burning or welding had been done the last thing I needed was the guilt of having nearly sunk a frigate!! I cannot say I was sad to leave the *Lynx* because by this time she was just a shadow of her former glory. We did not even sleep on her as there was no on board power, generators from the dockside provided this and if you had to do night shift duties, as in checking bilge water levels we had to sleep in a porta cabin on the jetty.

From time to time equipment on *Lynx* was restored to operational standard. One very important occasion occurred on 28 June 1977 she was at Spithead for Queen's Silver Jubilee Fleet Review *Lynx*, was manned by members of the Royal Navy Reserve, and HMS Wildfire at Chatham and as such represented the Royal Navy Reserve Fleet. She returned to Chatham on 1 July 1977. A few months later during a Royal visit to Chatham Dockyard on Friday 9 December 1977 the Duke of Edinburgh toured *Lynx* for twenty minutes.

In 1980 *Lynx's* upper deck was open to the public at that year's Navy Days held over the May Bank Holiday weekend. Thousands of visitors toured the ship, which was being prepared for the mothball fleet. *Lynx* was being used for trials and as such made occasional trips to sea, one such occurred on 6 June 1980 when *Lynx* left Basin 3 to venture into the River Medway at 09.20 in the morning. The following year, *Lynx* was declared surplus to requirements and placed on the disposal list in March. Many expected to see the old frigate being towed away to the scrapyard, but were relieved when; the Bangladeshi Navy bought *Lynx*.

She sailed from Chatham Dockyard, which had been her home since mid 1974 on 1 March 1982 and made for Portsmouth. After being refurbished she was transferred to the Bangladeshi Navy in a ceremony held on 12 March 1982 and extensively refitted before her transfer. In Bangladesh the ship bares the name of *Abu Bakr*

At the time of writing *Abu Bakr* was still in service with the Bangladeshi Navy and used in a training capacity. *Abu Bakr* is; however, likely to be reduced to reserve and probably scrapped within the next few years.

LLANDAFF

Built by R & W Hawthorn Leslie and Co Ltd at Hebburn on Tyne. *Llandaff* was laid down on 27 August 1953 and launched on 30 November 1955 by Countess Mountbatten of Burma. Five months later, however, whilst at her moorings in the River Tyne, *Llandaff* broke free during a gale and before she was brought under control she had struck the cruiser *Bermuda,* the new frigate *Russell* and a merchant ship. Not a particularly auspicious start to her Naval career.

On 15 January 1958 Commander I M V Browne became *Llandaff's* first commanding officer. After repairs were carried out, her construction continued and was eventually completed in April 1958. Her builder's trials were carried out around the Tyne before sailing for Portsmouth. The next few months saw the frigate carrying out her Royal Navy trials and spent a great deal of her time transiting between Portsmouth, Portland and Devonport. *Llandaff* left Devonport on 29 April for Portsmouth, where she would remain through until 7 May. Having been accepted into service she sailed up the Irish Sea and made for Londonderry where the newest frigate in the fleet took part in *Exercise Fresh Wind* until 6 July when she arrived at Plymouth for a four-day self-maintenance period.

Llandaff's first foreign visit started on 11 July when she arrived at Rotterdam for a six-day courtesy call. July also saw visits to Torbay and Barry before arriving back at Devonport on 29 July. Some of the crew were granted seasonal leave, whilst those left behind smartened the ship in preparation for the expected large crowds at that year's Navy Days, at which *Llandaff* was expected to be a star attraction. On the open days at the Naval Base, *Llandaff* was indeed one of the most popular exhibits, so much so that a contemporary report stated that one officer publicly stating. "This is the first ship they see and they all pile on. There are plenty of other ships here with hardly anyone on them."

Following this success, it was back to normal Naval order in the beginning of September when *Llandaff* had returned to Portland. She left the Dorset Naval Base on 26 September and sailed to Milford Haven and a return visit to the Welsh port of Barry on 3

October. After four very enjoyable days being treated to Welsh hospitality, *Llandaff* slipped and made the short trip back to Devonport.

On 9 October Commander I F O Alford became *Llandaff's* commanding officer. He presided over a short maintenance period that was finished just days before the frigate's departure on 22 October. After another round of training at Milford Haven and Portland, *Llandaff* arrived at Portsmouth on 28 October. Her stay would only be a few hours before she slipped and sailed for a planned visit to Belfast on 7 December. A period of intensive crew training followed in Northern Irish waters before the warship returned to Devonport on 22 December. Christmas leave was granted to the crew and she did not put to sea again until 26 January 1959.

First port of call was on 31 January when the frigate arrived at Las Palmas. She would later visit Gibraltar before moving onto Malta. When she left Malta, along with a number of other Royal Navy warships she headed to sea to take part in the large *Exercise Dawn Breeze 4.* The exercise ended on 24 March *Llandaff* left to return to Devonport, which was reached the following day.

Almost two months were spent in the dockyard that included the Easter period, before *Llandaff* left Devonport on 1 May and arrived at Portsmouth the same day. Her next foreign visit was to Copenhagen. She arrived at the port on 8 May and after sailing through 'Kronloebet' she tied up alongside. Copenhagen was a marvellous city to explore on foot, many of the men onboard the frigate taking full advantage of the cultural delights, whilst others onboard quickly found the local hostels. After five days *Llandaff* slipped back into the North Sea to conduct exercises there and in the Western Approaches until 22 May when she visited Brest. Another to Lisbon followed this visit on 28 May. Upon her arrival at Gibraltar on 6 June she transferred to the Mediterranean Fleet on 8 June. Three days later the frigate returned to sea to take part in *SARDEX* and a port of call was paid to Palmas Bay. She then crossed the Mediterranean sailing through the Suez Canal and Red Sea before joining forces with other warships in the Indian Ocean for *Exercise Jet*, which was based on the Pakistani port of Karachi. She left on 13 August to visit Trincomalee and Singapore.

Llandaff spent the remainder of 1959 in the Far East and spent Christmas spent there too. Over the course of the first three months of 1960 she continued a busy schedule of port visits and exercises before starting her journey home to the United Kingdom. On 25 March she arrived at Gibraltar and transferred to the Home Fleet. Whilst at the colony she prepared for her participation in *Exercise Dawn Breeze V*, which lasted until 1 April, with her return to Devonport. She soon entered into the dockyard and work started on the frigate, whilst her crew enjoyed a period of leave.

Commander I R Bowden, *Llandaff's* latest commanding officer boarded his new command on 11 May. The frigate would remain in dockyard hands until early November when *Llandaff* slipped from Devonport and put to sea for post refit trials, many of these were conducted in the waters off Portland. On 10 November she visited Cardiff and the crew made a visit to the nearby city of Llandaff.

November was spent conducting crew training and saw a brief visit to Portsmouth before returning to Devonport on 10 December. Christmas leave was granted and upon the crew's return in the New Year preparations began in earnest for the ships next Far East deployment. On 5 January 1961 *Llandaff* began her journey to join the Far East Station, which for the second year in a row saw her taking part in *Exercise Jet* in the waters off Trincomalee in early March. On St Patrick's Day she secured alongside in the Navy Base at Singapore, before continuing her journey to Hong Kong.

After another spell at Singapore, *Llandaff* visited Karatsu, Hong Kong and Yokohama. Yokohama is sited on the northwestern edge of Tokyo Bay and edged by gently rolling hills. The attractions of downtown Tokyo, however, were more alluring, than anything to be found locally in the port and many organised trips were organised to Japan's capital city. *Llandaff* visited the Perhentian Islands in early July and her south sea odyssey continued after a maintenance period at Singapore with visits to Penang and Lumut before returning to Singapore on 22 July 1961.

Late July saw *Llandaff* at Aden and Bahrain, before operating in the Persian Gulf in support of Royal Navy warships operating against the feared Iraqi invasion of neighbouring Kuwait. *Llandaff* remained in the Persian Gulf until 21 August when she headed south for Mombassa, where she arrived eight days later. She remained there until 17 September. After a two-day stop over at Pemba and a slightly longer stay at Mombassa, *Llandaff* returned to the Persian Gulf by the end of September.

Llandaff carried out a tour of ports in the region and at each was greeted by local dignitaries and extended the hand of friendship of the British government. Some of the ports visited in October included Bahrain, Kor Kuwai, Port Sudan and Aden. On 27 October she started her northerly overnight transit of the Suez Canal and entered the Mediterranean the next day.

Three days later she arrived at Malta, where *Llandaff* was docked down until 13 November. Essential maintenance had been carried out on the frigate and following some days spent at sea to correct any outstanding defects, *Llandaff* slipped out of Malta and headed for Gibraltar. After two days at Gibraltar her journey to Portsmouth resumed, where she arrived on 1 December. Her stay was only brief as after a few days she sailed for Devonport and the start of a lengthy refit.

She re-commissioned on May 10 1962 at Devonport with Commander Stephen Alexander Stuart RN in command. Commander Stuart joined the Royal Navy as a seaman in 1944 and obtained a special entry Cadet-ship to the Royal Naval College, Dartmouth. In 1945 he joined the cruiser *Belfast* in the BEF. He subsequently served as a sub lieutenant in the cruiser *Newcastle* and in small ships in the Mediterranean and New Zealand Stations and in Coastal Forces before specialising in gunnery in 1952. He was with the staff of the 8th Destroyer Squadron during the Korean War.

On commissioning *Llandaff* formed part of the 6th Frigate squadron. After work ups at Devonport where the main excitement was the operational tow of another frigate which had come to a halt in thick fog near the Shambles Rock, the squadron set sail for the Far East in August. On the way the ship took part in *Exercise Riptide III* and spent a two-week maintenance period at Trincomalee.

On 21 September she arrived at Singapore for an eight-day stay before travelling across the sea-lanes to Hong Kong, where she put into port on 5 October. The colony was home to the frigate for seven days before *Llandaff* retraced her route back to Singapore.

After a short stay at Singapore *Llandaff* arrived at Hong Kong in October in company with *Ark Royal* and *Rothesay*.

Trouble had been brewing in Aden for many years and during 1962 a rebellion broke out. A ship with excellent radar capability was required and *Llandaff* was detached to support British forces in the area.

Whilst at Aden on December 8, a merchant ship lying at the fuelling berth next to *Llandaff* burst into flames and within ten minutes the frigate had fire-fighting teams onboard who brought the flames under control. *Llandaff* left the port the same day and after twelve days at sea finally put into port at Penang. Seven days were spent alongside, with the crew enjoying the tropical heat and the various pleasures found ashore. Christmas Day was spent onboard the frigate with all the usual festive fare, although the surroundings were of a far more exotic nature than many were accustomed to. All good port visits come to an end, and this one did on 27 December when *Llandaff* returned to Singapore the next day.

1963 started for *Llandaff* with Royal Duty. On 1 January *Llandaff* acted as safety ship during the Queen's flight from Canada via Fiji en route to New Zealand and Australia and in so doing the ship covered 12,000 miles in six weeks with only six days in harbour. Visits were subsequently made to Fiji, Suva and Port Moresby. She left the latter destination on 12 February and made for Singapore.

On 2 March the frigate arrived at the tropical island of Langkawi for *Exercise Jet*, which continued for two days before the ship was called away to attempt to catch pirates off Tawau. Having had some degree of success in this task, *Llandaff* returned to Singapore on 18 March and was docked down until 1 April.

When the frigate returned to service one of her first foreign visits was to Batu Batu, the Philippines Navy Base. Officers from the two navies toured each others ships and exchanged token gifts. The ship returned to Singapore at the end of March and then to Hong Kong and a further week off Tawau. The squadron returned to the United Kingdom via Colombo, Aden, Malta and Gibraltar finally arriving at Devonport on July 4 1963.

Following a brief refit she sailed on 12 August to take part in *Exercise Riptide 4*. After the successful exercise *Llandaff* briefly returned to her home base before carrying out the second of three planned summertime exercises in home waters. *Exercise Union* started on 2 September and took a total of ten days. This was followed by *JSC 126* two days later. On 28 September *Llandaff* sailed past Plymouth Hoe and secured inside the dockyard.

The rapid progress of technology was demonstrated in early October when between 7 and 30 October *Llandaff* was one of the escorts for the brand new nuclear powered submarine *Dreadnought*. The government was very cautious about this latest addition to the fleet and gave the project the highest security possible, hence the *Llandaff's* presence as escort for the submarine's first visit to Portsmouth. This was followed by a visit to Funchal and on 1 November she arrived for a docking period at Portsmouth.

On 21 November one of the high spots of the Home Leg of the commission was the ships' visit to Cardiff. The Welsh City of Llandaff was again visited by representatives from the frigate as was the city of Cardiff. Following a hugely successful visit *Llandaff* returned to Devonport for repairs that were completed during the period of Christmas leave.

With the return of the crew from their vacations, the ship's first visit of 1964 was to the Channel Islands and in particular to the largest of the islands, Jersey. *Llandaff* then took part in the six-day exercise *Exercise Vendetta*, until 19 January. This was quickly followed by *Operation Phoenix*, which came to an end on 6 February when she arrived at Gibraltar. After having crossed the Mediterranean the frigate arrived at Suez Canal on 12 February and following an incident free transit arrived at Aden on 16 February.

Llandaff sailed south and on 9 March arrived at Mombassa for an extended visit lasting eight-days, before sailing on St Patrick's Day for Aden. In June upon her return home *Llandaff* entered into long refit at Devonport, but not before being present at that year's Navy Days in August, albeit not open to the public.

The refit was completed in early April 1966 with *Llandaff* re-commissioning on 2 April 1966 at No 1 jetty at Devonport. Among those present was Commodore P E I Bailey,

Commodore HMS *Drake* and Commander Colin Marr, the latest commanding officer of the frigate.

Following trials at Devonport and Portland throughout the summer, *Llandaff* slipped out of Devonport on 19 September for Gibraltar at the start of her first Beira patrol. *Llandaff* paid visits to Malta, Suez and Aden before arriving at Mombassa on 12 October. Except for maintenance *Llandaff* remained on patrol in the Mozambique Channel until 7 November. Having been relieved on the patrol *Llandaff* sailed for Singapore and almost a week later the frigate anchored off the island of Gan, where she restocked her supplies and topped up her fuel, before continuing onto Singapore.

In the Far East, *Llandaff* was to spend a lot of time exercising with the aircraft carrier *Victorious* in between port visits to Singapore and Hong Kong. Christmas 1966 was spent at Hong Kong before spending the first part of January and February 1967 with *Victorious* again. On 3 February 1967 *Llandaff* arrived at Manila, where she prepared for more exercises with *Victorious* and *Leopard*.

On 12 February the exercises finished and *Llandaff* sailed to Singapore, where she arrived the following day. After just three days alongside she slipped out to sea and together with the *Leopard*, *Llandaff* arrived at Bangkok on 17 February for a five-day visit to the city. She then took to sea for Flag Officers Training Exercise (*FOTEX*), which took place from late February until 18 March.

The next month on 3 April *Llandaff* arrived at Singapore for a docking and defects period. The whole of April was spent in dockyard hands and the frigate only put to sea on 16 May. After five days at sea she arrived at Gan, en route for Mombassa and the Beira Patrol on which she maintained the Royal Navy's presence until 20 June, with an occasional port visit to Mombassa for crew rest. Later in July, when the ship was back at sea and on passage to the Seychelles *Llandaff* went to the assistance of the Liberian registered tanker *Conchita*.

When *Llandaff* arrived on the scene she embarked the Captain and three officers from the stricken ship before she sank. Seventeen-crew-members had already been rescued by the German ship *Drachenfels* and were later transferred to the *Llandaff*.

Llandaff arrived at the beautiful Seychelles Island chain on 7 July, for what proved to be a most enjoyable five days. Sailors from all departments on the warship spent many happy hours on the golden white sands, whilst others tried their hand at snorkelling and big fish angling. *Llandaff* left this paradise on 11 July and returned back to Mombassa to resume the boredom of the Beira patrol. This occupied the frigate until 18 August. After a short time at Mombassa and a brief visit to Gan, *Llandaff* arrived at Singapore on 6 September for another maintenance period, which would last for ten days. On 18 September 1967 the frigates' latest commanding officer, Commander I B Lennox was welcomed onboard by officers and crew.

Llandaff next ventured to sea on 2 October when she left for shakedown trials, which lasted until 13 October. *Llandaff* was declared fully operational and visited Hong Kong on 11 December remaining there for almost the entire month, only leaving on 29 December after Christmas celebrations onboard the frigate.

Upon her return to Singapore, *Llandaff* was again alongside conducting a self-maintenance period through until 12 February 1968. Another week was spent alongside preparing for her next deployment with the first of many port visits being Hong Kong on 23 February.

A few months later saw one of the deployment's highlights with the beginning of a Japanese tour. On 11 April *Llandaff* sailed into the port of Kagoshima. Many amongst the frigate's crew were taken aback by the warmth and generosity of the Japanese who extended every courtesy to the visiting sailors wherever they went. Second port on the Japanese tour was Nagasaki, which twenty-three years earlier had been the location of the second atomic bomb dropped on Imperial Japan during the closing stages of World War Two. Lots of the crew visited the shrine set up to honour the thousands who had died that day. *Llandaff* sailed from Nagasaki on 26 April and four days later took part in *Exercise Guile*. The exercise finished on 10 May but only two days later the second in the series of exercises with local naval forces commenced, this was called *Exercise Tamaraw*. *Llandaff* returned to Singapore on 10 June and remained there for the rest of June.

The first day of July saw the ship leave Singapore for the start of her return journey to the United Kingdom. Instead of sailing west through the Indian Ocean and the Suez Canal to get home, *Llandaff* was to sail across the Pacific, visiting numerous South Sea Islands, the United States and the Caribbean before arriving home. The crew were excited about this prospect and started out with high hopes for an excellent series of port visits. The first was in Australia, when on 9 July *Llandaff* sailed into Cairns. Ports of call to the Solomon Isles, New Zealand, Suva, Rotuma and Tarawa followed this before arriving at Pearl Harbor on 15 August.

Only two days were spent in Hawaii before the ship started off once more across the Pacific heading for the California coastline. After seven days steaming *Llandaff* arrived off Monterey and a couple of days later pulled into the US Navy base at Long Beach. There the British sailors were befriended by their American counterparts and challenged to a variety of sporting and leisure activities during the frigate's stay, which came to an end on 5 September.

Having passed through the Panama Canal, calls were made to Bridgetown and Porto Delgada before arriving at Devonport on 21 September. Soon after, *Llandaff* was taken in hand for a lengthy refit, which was not completed until 21 February 1969. The frigate spent the next few months working up in preparation for full operational status with frequent visits to Portland, Portsmouth and occasionally to Dartmouth.

On 28 May *Llandaff* paid a two-day visit to the Channel Island of Guernsey before returning to Devonport Dockyard. She left port on 16 June for some exercises. June saw visits to Harwich and nearby HMS *Ganges* and the Dutch Navy base at Den Helder. 1969 was a year that was full of pomp and ceremony. The ordination of Prince Charles as Prince of Wales saw Royal Navy warships with Welsh connections required to act as escort to the Royal Yacht *Britannia* during the course of a brief tour of Welsh ports. *Llandaff*, therefore, together with the destroyer *Glamorgan* escorted the Royal Yacht throughout late June and into early July on visits to Llandudno and Cardiff.

After a period spent operating as a surface target and adversary for submarine officers training and navigational training *Llandaff* sailed into Portsmouth harbour on 18

July for a brief stay. She slipped to take part in one of the largest reviews of warships for many years. The Western Fleet Assembly was held off Torquay and included ships ranging from the aircraft carrier *Eagle* and nuclear submarine *Valiant* to frigates such as *Llandaff*, over fifty ships were arranged in neat lines for inspection by HM Queen Elizabeth II. At the end of the review *Llandaff* and a large number of the visiting ships sailed into Devonport on 29 July.

A month was spent at Devonport during which minor modifications were made and general repairs were undertaken. Her first port of call upon leaving the Naval Base was at Gibraltar, which was reached on 1 September. During the next two months *Llandaff* operated in the Mediterranean and participated in a number of exercises with local navies. For the crew, however, the highlights were the port visits, which included Malta, Cassis and a return visit to Malta on 19 September. Three days later she sailed to take part in *Exercise Diamond Blue* between 23 and 27 September before again returning to Malta.

Llandaff's return journey to the United Kingdom was after an eight-day stay at Gibraltar. Her next landfall was another eight days later when she arrived at Faslane for training with submarines and other surface vessels. Later she crossed the Irish Sea and operated in the waters around Northern Ireland as part of the Londonderry Squadron. Politicians, however, had decided that the squadron was to be disbanded and as a result together with the frigate *Phoebe*, *Llandaff* became individual members of the Western Fleet Flotilla.

After spending some days at Devonport, November was spent shuttling between Portland, Portsmouth and Devonport. On 28 November she visited Amsterdam for a couple of days. On 2 December *Llandaff* entered Devonport and remained there over the Christmas and New Year period, with most of her crew having been granted seasonal leave. The beginning of 1970 was spent in the Clyde or Faslane areas before visiting Bergen in Norway on 14 January during a period on the fishery patrol. *Llandaff* also paid a couple of visits to Tromso during January. The frigate's long range diesels were ideally suited to this task, whilst her air direction role became secondary during the fishery patrols. This was followed by a period spent in the Londonderry Exercise areas before arriving at Devonport on 5 February for maintenance, which lasted until 13 March. During this time alongside, the frigate's latest commanding officer, Commander R A Snow assumed command on 10 February. Commander Snow had spent a large part of his early life in South Africa including part of his education at the South African Nautical College. In 1952 he joined the Royal Navy and within ten years had been promoted to the command of the minesweeper *Kirkliston*. Around this time he chose navigation as his speciality and went onto be promoted further until he assumed command of *Llandaff*.

She carried out trials and evaluations in and around Portland well into March and on 19/20 March was at Portland when, she was visited by Admiral Sir William O'Brien as Commander in Chief, Western Fleet. The end of the month saw a return to Devonport dockyard for another period in dock, which lasted until 22 June. After which, the short sea trip to Portsmouth was undertaken. All these preparations were leading to the ship being declared operational and for her eventual deployment to the Far East, which started on 30 June when she slipped from Portsmouth.

With the closure of the Suez Canal, *Llandaff* sailed around the Cape visiting Gibraltar, Freetown and Simonstown before starting a month long Beira patrol on 1 August. On 3 September she arrived at the island of Farquhar, which was followed by a refuelling stop at Gan and an arrival at Singapore on 12 September. *Llandaff* remained alongside until 5 October, which allowed her crew time off to relax.

Llandaff slipped from Singapore and set a course for Hong Kong, which after four days steaming was reached on the morning of 9 October. Three days later the frigate played an active role in *Exercise Far Flung*, which occupied the crew's full attention until 19 October. Late October saw more visits to Hong Kong, Manila and Subic Bay before returning to Hong Kong on 2 December. Whilst she was in the colony, severe weather conditions, so prevalent in the area, started to grow. On Friday 13 November the frigate's meteorological office reported the danger posed by Typhoon Joan and her sister storm, Typhoon Kate. These tropical storms caused a great deal of damage and destruction in the Bay of Bengal.

Llandaff slipped away from Hong Kong on 28 November and visited the American base at Okinawa, before returning to Hong Kong briefly, en route to Singapore and another maintenance period. This lasted until 30 January 1971. Forty wives and loved ones had flown out to be with their men-folk over the Christmas period and upon the ships' departure returned home on a scheduled flight.

February was a particularly busy month with two large exercises to undertake, *FEBEX 1* was quickly followed by *FEBSPORT*. By 26 February the frigate had arrived back at Singapore, where a further spell of maintenance was conducted until 8 March. For many the highlight of the Far East deployment was a visit to Japan, which occurred two days later when three-days were spent at the port of Nagasaki. Having left behind the wonderful Japanese hospitality on 13 March *Llandaff* sailed south to visit the northern Australian city of Darwin, before crossing to Christmas Island on 26 March. Late March saw an arrival at the Cocos Islands, whilst in April *Llandaff* arrived at Mauritius. Crowds thronged the dockside of Port Louis, Mauritius to watch the colourful ceremonial as the Governor General (Lord Williams) prepared to take passage in *Llandaff* to the island of Rodriques on a three day official visit. During the stay the ship's company', provided film shows for the populace ashore and were beaten at soccer by a team from the island.

Two days were spent on the small forty square mile island of Rodriques and the opportunity was taken for many of the crew to undertake local community work, such as repairing roofs and the painting of buildings on the islands. After performing his official duties, Lord Williams rejoined the *Llandaff* and the frigate returned him to Mauritius.

After all the pomp and ceremony a stint on the Beira patrol came as a boring aside. *Llandaff's* time on the patrol started on 16 April, thankfully only ten days were spent on patrol before starting the journey homewards. *Llandaff* was due back in the United Kingdom at the end of May and after calls to Simonstown and Gibraltar, the warship sailed passed Plymouth breakwater on 27 May flying her paying off pennant. Two days later Commander Snow presented a cheque for £201 to Longcause School in Plympton St Maurice. The money was raised whilst in the Far East.

On 13 September *Llandaff* was towed from Devonport to Chatham, where she soon entered the Standby Squadron and awaited her next period of activity in the fleet. In the event she only spent ten months in reserve before being brought back into service.

Llandaff's latest commander was Commander William Corry who was present when the frigate re-commissioned from Reserve at Chatham in June 1972 with visits to Harwich, Margate, Dover and Den Helder. Prior to taking up command of *Llandaff*, Commander Corry had been in command of the frigate *Keppel* and the officer in charge of the Reserve ships Unit at Chatham. He had also held a number of shore assignments after serving in the Far East, the Mediterranean during the Suez Crisis and at NAS Bawdy and the Wessex Division of the Royal Naval Reserve.

For her visits to Harwich and Dover *Llandaff* flew the flag of the Flag Officer Medway, Rear Admiral Colin Dunlop who paid official visits to the Mayors of both towns and at Harwich was host at a luncheon party held onboard the frigate. He also inspected HMS Ganges. *Llandaff* returned to Chatham so that further refitting could be undertaken. Commander Corry's term in command was a brief one as on 5 March Commander P D Deller assumed command and the ship herself finally re-commissioned at Chatham on 25 May 1973. The crew of *Llandaff* must have been getting used to a rapid change of commanders throughout the trials period and another change occurred on 27 September 1973.

Commander John S Kelly MBE assumed command of *Llandaff* and continued the trials program started by his predecessors. These trials were carried out in the waters around Chatham and the Thames Estuary, *Llandaff* sailed from Chatham Dockyard on 23 November for Portsmouth. More trials were undertaken before returning to Chatham on 21 December 1973, where Christmas leave was granted to the crew.

Work up and Shakedown was a drawn out affair that continued well into 1974. On 19 March *Llandaff* sailed into Portsmouth before becoming Gibraltar guard-ship until 11 April. During her time as guard-ship the frigate made a couple of excursions across the Straits to the port of Tangiers. Upon her return to Gibraltar she resumed her role as guard-ship until 25 April. The frigates' last few days at Gibraltar, were spent in preparation for the State Visit to London by Queen Margarethe of Denmark, which occurred on 29 April 1974.

The *Llandaff* fired a 21-gun salute on meeting the Danish Royal Yacht, *Danneborg* and manned and cheered ship before escorting the *Danneborg* and two minelayers to the overnight anchorage at Gravesend. Early next morning the *Llandaff* led the formation passed the Royal Naval College at Greenwich, where Queen Margarethe disembarked. *Llandaff* continued up the River Thames to secure alongside the cruiser *Belfast* in the Pool of London.

After a very successful visit, *Llandaff* sailed on 1 May to Rosyth. Five days later she participated in *JMC 742* until 20 May. Together with the cruiser *Blake*, *Llandaff* visited Gothenburg in Sweden. The visit was a fantastic success and even more so for *Llandaff*, when they won a tug of war contest with her much larger consort. The crew of *Blake* obviously did not like losing to a mere frigate and turned their powerful flight deck fire hoses on the frigate moored alongside.

On 30 May *Llandaff* returned to Chatham for a maintenance period, which was finished on 4 July. The next day she slipped and arrived at Portsmouth. A period at Portland followed which was spent preparing the ship and her crew for another spell East of Suez.

Llandaff's course took her around the Cape and into the Indian Ocean. Routine patrol duties were occasionally interrupted with very pleasant activities, such as collecting seashells on the white sand beaches of the Seychelles. *Llandaff's* programme allowed a week on these jewels in a turquoise sea. The visit started in considerable style with the Chief Minister, James Mancham and the actor Peter Sellers attending the official cocktail party onboard the frigate. Others onboard the frigate tried out all sorts of activities, divers dived off St Ann's Island and the young seaman's divisions, banyanned, a group of sailors, led by AB Brownrigg, helped renovate some poor people's homes.

Later, *Llandaff* during a visit to Mombassa, whilst the ship undertook a maintenance period some of the crew took the opportunity to visit Nairobi for a long weekend. After a visit to Mauritius over the last week of October and into November, the warship resumed her Beira patrol duties until arriving at Simonstown on 22 November.

Six days later she was back at sea en route to Gibraltar and the opportunity was taken for some weapons training whilst underway. After a lengthy period at sea, Gibraltar was reached on 13 December before sailing for Chatham, where she arrived on 19 December, in time for Christmas leave to be granted to the crew.

Llandaff stayed at Chatham until 10 February 1975 when she slipped and made her way to Portsmouth. After leaving Portsmouth first port of call was at Gibraltar to take part in a series of NATO exercises that culminated in the large exercise entitled *Spring Ex.*. In all some sixteen Royal Navy warships and auxiliaries visited Gibraltar over a ten-day period. Ships taking part were *Llandaff, Leopard, Ajax, Ashanti, Charybdis, Dido, Fife, Glamorgan, Hermione, Jupiter, Norfolk, Nubian, Onyx, Olympus, Rothesay, Reliant, Black Rover* and *Tidereach*. At the end of *Spring Ex*, the ships moved into the Mediterranean and *Llandaff*, visited the port of Cagliari, before returning to Gibraltar on 14 March.

After crossing the English Channel and paying an overnight stay at Portland on St Patrick's Day, *Llandaff* visited Cardiff docks three days later. During the visit, members of the ships-company left the ship to attend a Cathedral service at Llandaff Cathedral. The frigate left the Welsh port on 25 March and returned to Chatham Dockyard.

Another change of command occurred on 2 April 1975 when *Llandaff's* last commanding officer, Commander George Oxley assumed command. He took her out of the dockyard into the River Medway on 14 April. First port of call was at Dundee, after which the frigate conducted three days of weapons training. At its conclusion, *Llandaff* arrived at Portsmouth where she stayed until 28 April. The next day she returned to Chatham where she was docked down in one of the dockyard's dry docks from 3 May.

The sailors of *Llandaff* whilst at Chatham Dockyard, had to vote for a new Miss Llandaff to represent the crew from a dozen local girls. They eventually chose 18 year old Nicola Newcombe from Strood. Later, fourteen year old Christine De Looze of Chatham, who was wheelchair bound visited the ship and was given a transister radio from Commander G Oxley.

Llandaff sailed on 21 June for Portland and after spending some time at Portsmouth and Portland *Llandaff* together with *Glamorgan, Ajax* and *Plymouth, Llandaff* set off to the Far East. The trip east included the first transit of the Suez Canal by a large force of Royal Navy warships since the canal's closure in 1967. The group visited Gibraltar, Malta and Port Said. Whilst at Port Said, awaiting their turn to transit the great waterway a lucky few members of the crew were given a guided tour of the Pyramids.

Once through the canal temperatures in the Red Sea reached 105 degrees and did not fall below 90 at night. Those in the ship's engine room fared even worse with temperatures reaching up to 130 degrees. These conditions lingered until *Llandaff* entered the Gulf of Aden. Within twenty-four hours the full force of the monsoon season caught the ship and a long period of rough weather followed.

On 28 August *Llandaff* arrived at the bustling chaos of Bombay. The port was heaving with all manner of vessels from small boats to large container ships and the Royal Navy was frequently dwarfed by large oil tankers. Later together with *Ajax, Berwick* and *RFA Gold Rover she* visited Madras until 4 September. Later they joined up with the destroyer *Glamorgan* and the frigates *Plymouth, and Rothesay.* The tanker *Tidespring* and the supply ship *Tarbartness* supported the warships.

After sailing to Malaya the Royal Navy force continued to operate with friendly forces and in particular with the military of Australia and Malaysia, including a large number of fast-patrol boats. These exercises were followed by an arrival at Singapore on 10 September for a five-day rest.

Glamorgan, Tidespring and *Plymouth* stayed at Singapore while all the other ships including *Llandaff* sailed for Hong Kong, where they arrived on 19 September. Following maintenance, *Llandaff* arrived at Surabaya on 18 October. Later the frigate took part in Royal Australian Navy exercise *Swift Swing,* which started on 25 September and took the ships taking part from south of Bali across the Gulf of Carpentaria. From there the ships preceded south inside the Great Barrier Reef to Newcastle, New South Wales and Sydney. Later in the month the frigate was part of the Royal Navy's contribution to *Exercise TASMANEX 75. Exercise TASMANEX 75* lasted eleven days and involved two submarines as well as ships from the Royal Navy, Royal Australian Navy, New Zealand and the United States.

On 30 November *Llandaff* arrived at Auckland, where she remained until 8 December. A short sea voyage was undertaken the same day that saw the British frigate arrive in Napier for a short visit. December also saw port visits to Lyttleton and Tauranga where Christmas and New Year were celebrated in true South Sea style. On 5 January 1976 the frigate sailed from Tauranga to continue the cruise. *Llandaff* left the romantic island of Bali with mixed memories. Banyan barbecues were order of the day and thoroughly enjoyed by those who went ashore during the morning. The afternoon session was less successful following a downpour from a tropical storm.

In January *Llandaff* headed for Napier, North Island of New Zealand and then Lyttleton on the South Island. These visits were swiftly followed by a visit to the Cook Islands towards the end of January. While *Llandaff* spent four days at the Pacific Island of Raratonga, her duties made good use of the time to inspect the brilliantly coloured coral reef. When an old anchor believed to be from a World War Two tank landing craft was discovered, it was raised and presented to the islanders.

After stopping at Samoa *Llandaff* headed out into the Pacific for the long passage across the Pacific to the United States calling at Hawaii en route.

Passing under the Golden Gate bridge at San Francisco, *Llandaff* continued up river to Sacramento, the Capital of California and ninety miles inland to take part in America's Bicentennial celebrations. In Sacramento one of the main events was a linked religious service between Trinity Cathedral, Sacramento and Llandaff Cathedral in Wales. The time difference meant that the morning service in California co-incided with evensong in *Llandaff*. Whilst at Sacramento the crew fulfilled a full social and sporting programme which also included visits to Reno's casino's and the ski centre at the beautiful Lake Tahoe.

Having left Sacramento behind and sailed the 90 miles back out into the Pacific Ocean the eight Royal Navy warships took part in a five-nation exercise involving 38 ships, 200 aircraft and 18,000 men off the California coast from March 2 to 12 1976. British sailors joined American, Canadian, Australian and Kiwi's in *Exercise Valiant Heritage*, so called in recognition of the long-standing spirit of co-operation and mutual support among the countries involved.

Directed by the Commander of the US Third Fleet, the exercise was designed to test and improve combat readiness in all aspects of modern naval warfare, including anti submarine, anti ship and air defence. *Llandaff* returned to the Atlantic Ocean via the Panama Canal, despite a canal workers strike causing chaos at the entrance to the ship canal. She sailed into Portsmouth on April 14 before soon making the short journey to Chatham Dockyard. On 30 May *Llandaff* was opened to the public at Chatham Navy Days where thousands of people took the opportunity to tour the ship for the last time before her sale.

Another last chance to tour the ship was presented to the residents of Portsmouth at Navy Days in August. The following month *Lowestoft* and *Llandaff* sailed for weapons training in the Plymouth Area before *Lowestoft* was scheduled to take part in *Exercise Team Work*. During night exercises on September 6, *Lowestoft's* port side turbo alternator emitted a violent screaming noise seconds before disintegrating, sending clouds of smoke and steam throughout the ship. *Llandaff* stood by to assist and later towed *Lowestoft* part the way back to Plymouth, with the tug *Advice* completing the tow back into the dockyard.

The frigate said her farewell to Llandaff and Cardiff on a final visit to the city before paying off and to commemorate the strong links between ship and city. Commander George Oxley, *Llandaff's* commanding officer presented the ship's bell and ensign to Llandaff Cathedral on behalf of the ships company. The handing over ceremony took place in the Cathedral in the presence of Princess Margaret during the annual Seafarers service. The crew had previously lined the approach to the Cathedral for the arrival of the Princess.

After a full programme of sporting and social events, including a lunch hosted by the Lord Mayor of Cardiff and another given by the Dean and Chapter at the Cathedral, *Llandaff* sailed from Cardiff docks for the short journey to Barry, carrying a number of local dignitaries. Once clear of the docks *Llandaff* was finally able to fly her 250-foot long paying off pennant.

Llandaff was docked down at Chatham and her sonar was removed shortly before her sale to Bangladesh was confirmed. The Bangladeshi Navy asked for the equipment to be re-installed and the MOD agreed to a reduction in the purchase price of £1 million as a result of the mix up. On 10 December 1976 *Llandaff* was transferred to Bangladesh at a ceremony in London's Royal Albert Docks. She was renamed *Umar Farooq* and became the first warship in the fleet of Bangladesh. The frigate's pennant number was reversed, thus becoming F16.

Umar Farooq then sailed for Portsmouth, where she was visited by the Commander in Chief Naval Home Command, Admiral Sir Terence Lewin, who cut a special cake and received a ship's plaque from the frigate's new commanding officer, Captain M A Khan.

After loading extra equipment and sharing in the Dockyard's Christmas and New Year's celebrations, the officers and crew of *Umar Farooq* sailed from Portsmouth in mid February 1977 and set a course for Bangladesh. *Umar Farooq* has continued to serve in the Bangladeshi Navy since that date including invaluable work during the regions regular terrible floods, where she has been used to distribute humanitarian aid to those worst affected

HMS *Salisbury* at sea

(M Donoghue)

(M Donoghue)

HMS Salisbury

The Bridge of HMS *Salisbury*   *(M Donoghue)*

RFA *Retainer* fueling HMS *Salisbury* at sea   *(M Donoghue)*

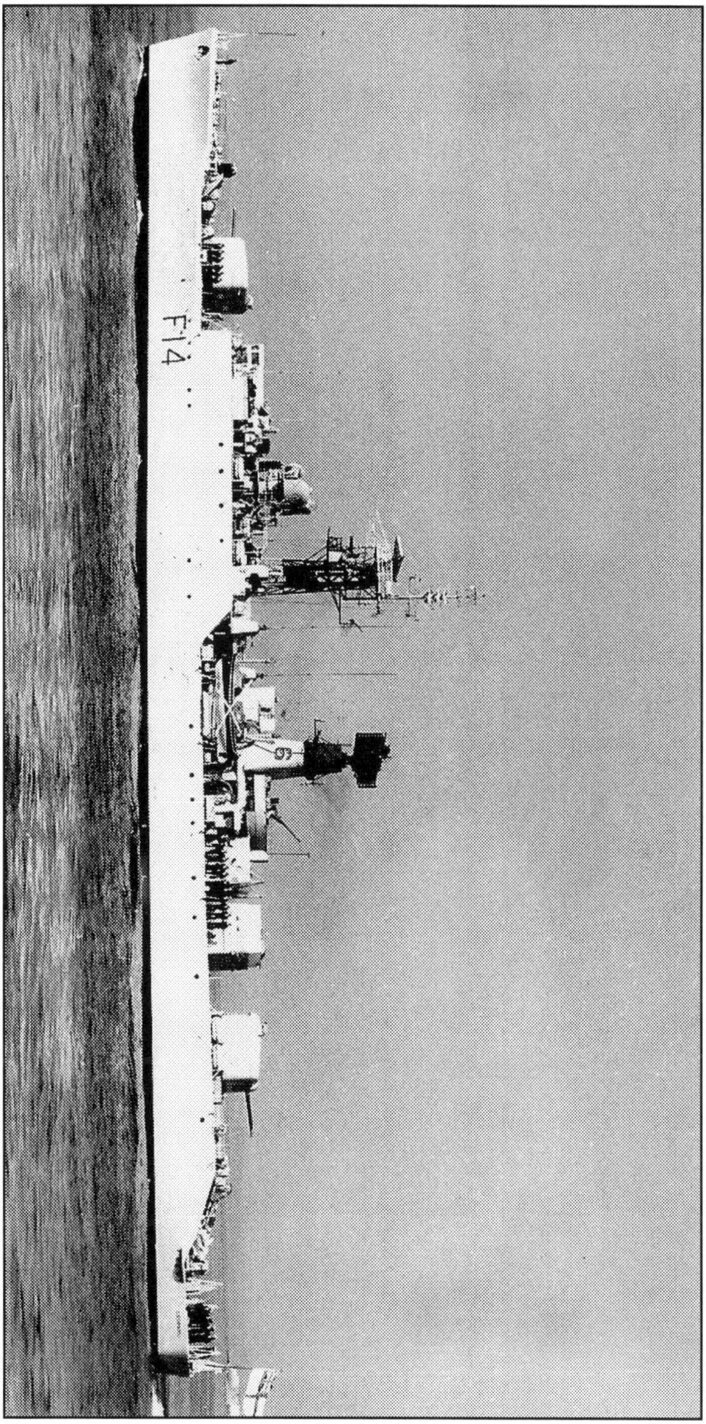

HMS *Leopard* (*Navpic*)

A great aerial shot of HMS *Chichester*

(*R Burton*)

HMS *Chichester* (R Burton)

Catching up on the news (R Burton)

Ships Company HMS *Chichester* Summer 1960

(*R Burton*)

HMS *Lynx* (*Navpic*)

HMS *Llandaff*

(Navpic)

HMS *Jaguar* (*Navpic*)

HMS *Puma*

(Navpic)

HMS *Puma*   *(Navpic)*

HMS *Lincoln*

(Navpic)

JAGUAR

Jaguar was ordered from William Denny and Bros Ltd in Dumbarton and was laid down as yard number 1476 on 2 November 1953 and launched on 20 July 1957 by Her Royal Highness Princess Alexandra of Kent. As the Princess broke the bottle of Champagne on the frigate's bow's, she was surprised to see nothing happening, the ship remained firmly on the slipway. After waiting a few moments the Princess gave a gentle push. This helping-hand, must have worked, as the ship then started down the way. Work on the frigate was relatively swift and she was finally completed and commissioned on 9 December 1959 and became the last warship to be built at the shipyard before it closed. Almost a year before on the 5 January 1959 Lt Commander M G Moberly had been appointed as the frigates' first commanding officer who oversaw her construction.

The ship was now under the command of Commander James Pertwee, RN and the White Ensign was appropriately hoisted. At 1550 on 9 December it was lowered again and she sailed the next day from the yard under the Red Ensign to swing compass and see what speed could be coaxed from her.

Two days later having returned to Dumbarton *Jaguar* was in the Clyde undergoing trials on all systems including stabilisers and all control functions were exhaustively checked and doubled checked by a Denny's trials team and by the Royal Navy. By the next evening all seemed well and at 1250 on the 12 December the Denny team were disembarked and *Jaguar* left the Firth of Clyde to go south into the Fleet.

Jaguar raced down the Irish Sea and during the passage a whip aerial broke. She anchored in the Solent on Monday 14 December. For those wanting to get ashore there was to be disappointment as the dockyard siren had blown and *Jaguar's* crew would have to wait until the next day to enter Portsmouth.

Jaguar spent Christmas at Portsmouth but the New Year promised a proper shakedown for the ship and crew. She sailed from Portsmouth on 7 January and spent the next two months ensuring everything onboard worked to specification. Unfortunately early in 1960, everything was not up to standard in the engine room of the latest Royal Navy frigate.

Jaguar spent another Sunday to take the trial's team back to Portsmouth on the 15th. Triplane Target Tracking exercises were carried out at Portland before returning to go alongside at Portsmouth on 19 February.

She was soon back at sea, however, and sailed to her home-port of Chatham. She sailed past Sheerness at 08.05 on 22 February and continued up the River Medway until she arrived at Chatham Dockyard's South Lock. Having been eased into the Dock Gates by the harbour tugs, *Jaguar* entered Basin 3 at the Dockyard for the first time. The crew and ship would under normal circumstances spend a short while in port before resuming her shakedown, this wasn't to be the case with *Jaguar*. The cause was discovered to be blasting grit in her main machinery. A Board of Inquiry was convened to uncover the root of the contamination and to make recommendations to remedy the situation. As if by comic irony, the ship was also used in this state by the 'Carry On' movie team to shoot scenes for the movie 'Watch Your Stern', adding insult to injury for the crew.

Her engine problems were never discussed when she was smartly presented at Chatham Navy Days between 16 and 18 April 1960 the ship welcomed onboard an impressive number of visitors; on the Saturday 4,600, on the Sunday 6,100 and on the Monday 5,500.

The damage inflicted by the grit was repaired at Portsmouth, where the opportunity was also taken to refit the ship. On 23 January 1961 a new commanding officer was welcomed onboard the frigate in the shape of Commander D T Goodhugh. It would, however, be some months before he took his new command to sea. The refit was finally completed on 3 June and the ship was taken to Portland to finally start her trials and work-up's.

On 30 June at 17.55 *Jaguar* was alongside the Battle class destroyer *Trafalgar* at Portland. Three days later at 13.00 *Jaguar* fired a 21-gun salute in honour of King Olaf of Norway's birthday. The Norwegian submarine *Ula* was in port at the time. The next day

Jaguar left port at 07.50 in the morning to visit the French port of Cherbourg. The French town's VIP's extended every courtesy to the ship and the crew during the one-day visit.

After this pleasant trip *Jaguar* made her way back to Portsmouth on 29 July via Portland. Twelve days were spent at the Naval Base before she slipped and returned to Chatham. Whilst at Chatham, maintenance was carried out and the ship was docked from 14 August. The maintenance was completed and the frigate was back at sea on 7 September. Her destination was South Africa, via Gibraltar and Freetown.

Jaguar arrived at Simonstown on 27 September in order to take part in *CAPEX* with sister-ship *Leopard*. On 21 October *Jaguar* visited Port Elizabeth for a two-day courtesy call. A privilege was bestowed on the frigate when she was selected to escort the Queen and Duke of Edinburgh in *Britannia* between 20 November and 6 December during the Royal tour to Takoradi, Monrovia, Freetown and Bathurst. The final port of call of the Royal Tour was Dakar, which was reached on 6 December. After the Queen had completed her official engagements, she returned to the Royal Yacht and left port with *Jaguar* acting as escort.

Jaguar parted company with *Britannia* and headed independently to Freetown and St Helena before arriving back at Simonstown on 20 December in time for the Christmas celebrations. The New Year started well and amongst many other exotic ports of call, the frigate paid a return call to Dakar. February saw a port of call paid to Freetown where she remained until late in the month. On 2 March *Jaguar* returned to Simonstown. From there she headed into the Indian Ocean four days later and after eleven days at sea, the ship finally arrived at the island of Mauritius. Five-days were spent at anchor off the island. The crew were allowed shore leave during these days and many tried out a variety of water sports, whilst others practised their cookery skills with barbecue's on the beach.

Jaguar arrived back at Simonstown on 29 March, where she remained until 24 April and arrived the same day at Capetown. Late April saw a visit to East London, whilst the following month *Jaguar* visited Port Elizabeth and Simonstown.

Spring and summer 1962 were spent exercising in South African and South American waters. She also undertook the duties of calling on British dependencies in the

South Atlantic area to dispense medical assistance and to provide a reassurance for the residents of these desolate islands that the Royal Navy was always nearby in case of emergency. Another reason for making the trip was to standby in the middle of the Atlantic to track the movements of Britain's first satellite, which had been launched some days before from Cape Canaveral.

On 3 July she arrived at Durban for a six-day visit, before returning to Simonstown. After a brief stopover, *Jaguar* sailed to cross the South Atlantic to visit ports in South America. Her first port of call was at the Uruguayan Capital City of Montevideo. She later went onto visit the Brazilian ports of Santos and the always colourful and cosmopolitan city of Rio de Janeiro on 11 August. Whilst in South America *Jaguar* received a call from the Commandant of the Brazilian Air Force Base at Camp Grande in the wild of Mato Grosso. He told *Jaguar* that their search for a big cat Jaguar was over. Juno who was later renamed Jason on account of a sexing error was one of two cubs captured when, their mother was shot by hunters. The Brazilian Air Force flew the cat to Rio for embarkation in the frigate.

With the Jaguar cub safely onboard the frigate, *Jaguar* sailed on 17 August and headed north en route to the United Kingdom via Las Palmas and Gibraltar. She sailed from Gibraltar on 1 September and arrived back at Portsmouth on 4 September. A great deal of press attention focussed on the big cat *Jaguar* had onboard before he was handed over to a zoo to look after him properly. Two days later she slipped and sailed for Chatham, where she arrived at 08.05 in the morning of 7 September. Ten days later she entered into a lengthy refit, which continued until 25 January 1963.

Jaguar remained close to Chatham Dockyard in the early months of 1963 except for a visit to Portsmouth in late February. On 29 May she sailed from Portland and remained in the Solent area. After a couple of days at Portsmouth and Portland she sailed to visit the German Navy at Kiel. Upon her return she took part in FOS/MC at the beginning of July. On 12 July *Jaguar* arrived at Chatham at 07.30.

After a brief period of leave *Jaguar* left Chatham on 12 August and following a quick work up joined a large American group for *Exercise Riptide IV* in the Bay of Biscay after which *Jaguar* sailed south. Her voyage to the Persian Gulf was planned to take in three one-day stops at Gibraltar, Malta and Aden. At Gibraltar, *Jaguar* had a opportunity to renew acquaintances with the South African frigate *SAS President Steyn*.

The summer heat in the Suez Canal was intense and *Jaguar's* crew, were happy to meet up with the destroyer *Diamond* at Port Tewfik. The destroyer passed over some hurricane fans to cool compartments within the frigate. *Jaguar* eventually reached Aden on September 5.

At Bahrain Captain, Amphibious Warfare Squadron (Captain M W B Kerr, DSC RN) was embarked for a big naval exercise. During these exercises *Jaguar's* controllable pitch screws came in useful when she was called upon to tow a 300 ton Rhino ferry to the landing which was to take place outside the Gulf, some 450 miles away.

After the exercises, *Jaguar* was again used to tow the vessel back to Bahrain. At Bahrain an Australian tramp steamer arrived and sliced three feet into the frigate's stern, whilst alongside the deep-water jetty. Repairs were made to the warship, which was not, fortunately, severely damaged in the incident.

The rest of the Middle East leg was spent with the aircraft carrier *Ark Royal* and *Plymouth* in two exercises at the mouth of the Gulf, before sailing to the Far East via Mombassa. All the *Midlink 6* ships, some 35 in all, including *Ark Royal* and the American 'carrier *USS Essex* were assembled in Karachi by November 1. This was an extensive exercise run for CENTO by the Pakistani Navy. The final day of the exercise coincided with the unpleasant news of the assassination of American President John F Kennedy, it was also the day that *Jaguar* sailed for South Africa.

After a short fuelling stop at Mombassa, Durban was reached for a short visit, before returning to Simonstown for three weeks over the Christmas period. There followed a short cruise up to East London and Mossel Bay before again returning to Simonstown.

David Knowles was onboard *Jaguar* during this period:

"After a short self-maintenance period, we made a few courtesy visits to Port Elizabeth, East London and Durban before crossing the South Atlantic to visit South America. The journey west took the ship to Tristan da Cunha where the local people requested help with the making of a coastal road. The captain accepted the challenge to move a rather large piece of rock that was causing problems. We bombarded the area with the main armament but I cannot recall whether it was successful or not. The islanders were grateful for our efforts and repaid us with a large amount of the biggest Crayfish you have ever seen. I thought they were Lobsters."

"A day or so after leaving Tristan da Cunha the ship struck a mysterious object sometime before midnight. After internal investigation, it was decided to make an external search with the ships divers but nothing was found. The conclusion was that we had hit a very large whale and with luck, simply woken the monster from its sleep."

"We then called into Port Stanley, Falkland Islands before making a visit to Rio de Janeiro. We arrived in the Brazilian port one-day early due to the Navigating Officer putting us in the wrong time zone, how embarrassing for the captain. A draft to ships on the SA & SA station was much sought after as the hospitality and runs ashore were normally excellent, and my trip fully lived up to expectation. The sauce on my dinner was the fact that I departed UK as a boy and came back a man after the older members of my mess took me ashore the first night in Rio and arranged a rather charming young lady for me. It was so good I went back for more the following night. In fact all week!"

Further visits were made to Punta Del Este, Mar Del Plata and Rio. On the way back to Simonstown, David Knowles recalls that at Simonstown the ship took part in exercises with the local navy units. "We then commenced a period of training and minor exercises with the South African navy. The exercises were of quite low intensity as the South African ships were not fully complemented and therefore had to anchor each night."

In April 1964 the frigates third commanding officer was welcomed onboard by the crew of the warship he was Commander J B Robatham. The ship continued to operate in her area of operations before starting the long journey home to the United Kingdom, where she arrived at 13.15 on 7 August at Chatham Dockyard. Soon after she entered into a lengthy refit. The frigate's fourth commanding officer, Commander T C Cotton was received onboard on 1 September. *Jaguar's* refit proceeded without any great incident and *Jaguar* re-commissioned at Chatham on January 8, 1965, HRH Princess Alexandra amongst the guests.

On 18 January *Jaguar* left Chatham Dockyard through the South Lock of the Bull Nose and after four days at sea arrived at Portsmouth, where she continued to work up prior to being declared fully operational on 5 February. The trials and work up's continued throughout the early months of 1965. She arrived at Portsmouth on April 4 and handed over a block of stone for Portsmouth Cathedral as a gift from the Mayor and Municipality of Simonstown and arrived at Chatham on 15 April for a short refit. On 17 May *Jaguar* sailed from Chatham Dockyard at one o'clock in the afternoon and started her deployment to the South Atlantic.

On 9 June *Jaguar* arrived at Rio de Janeiro for a six-day visit. She arrived at Simonstown on 25 June to replace sister ship *Leopard* on station. July saw visits to Durban and Simonstown, whilst at the beginning of August the frigate arrived at Diego Suarez. *Jaguar's* packed itinerary continued with ports of call paid to Port Louis, the island of Rodriquez, St Brandon, Agalega, another to Port Louis before visiting Mombassa on 24 September.

The ship acquired three extra guns in her armament, following a diving expedition, whilst in the Mozambique Straits. Leave was granted to swimming parties at a small coral reef and three cannon encrusted with coral were recovered from the seabed. Unfortunately, the name of the ship wrecked on the reef, was not forthcoming. The only letters that were visible were 'MA___TE'.

On 1 October she arrived at Simonstown, where the ship received maintenance for ten days before staying in Simonstown area until 12 November. A brief spell at sea was followed by a fairly lengthy period at Simonstown, where she remained until 16 December, when she slipped for a four-day visit to Port Elizabeth. *Jaguar* spent Christmas and New Year at Simonstown. *Jaguar* left Simonstown to visit South America on 10 January.

Jaguar arrived at Porto Belgrano in Argentina on 24 January. She spent some time operating with Argentine units and the crew spent many enjoyable hours playing football against teams from the Argentinean armed forces. After four days the frigate slipped and sailed north to visit the Argentine Capital City of Buenos Aires. In February *Jaguar* visited Punta del Este, Port Stanley, Deception Island and Valparaiso, whilst March started with a 12 March appointment to visit the port of Guayaquil.

On 18 March *Jaguar* arrived at Panama City, just prior to crossing from the Pacific Ocean and into the Caribbean via the Panama Canal on 20 March. After five days at sea, *Jaguar* arrived at the jewel in the Caribbean that is Bermuda. The visit would be a very short overnight stay at anchor, before resuming her journey back to Portsmouth, where she arrived on 4 April. She spent the night alongside, before sailing the next day for Chatham and secured within the dockyard at midday.

Jaguar was due a refit, which was scheduled to start on 2 May 1966, however, the refit was delayed a couple of months because of operational commitments within the dockyard. Once the refit started in earnest the ship was essentially stripped down for a complete overhaul of all systems and compartments. Commander P W Greening was appointed as *Jaguar's* latest commanding officer on 31 July 1967.

In October 1967 *Jaguar* completed her 18-month modernisation at Chatham which improved her radar and radio capabilities and enhanced her outward appearance by the addition of a new mainmast which also housed her funnel uptakes for four of her eight engines. On 21 October *Jaguar* re-commissioned into the fleet with the ceremony being attended by Vice Admiral and Mrs Parker. Two days later *Jaguar* left Chatham Dockyard and spent the next week at sea conducting trials. She returned to base on 1 November.

Jaguar left Chatham at 16.20 a week later to visit Portsmouth, where on 14 December she was declared operational to the fleet. Upon her return to Chatham on 19 December *Jaguar's* crew left the ship for seasonal leave. Upon their return in the early days of 1968, the ship was brought back to life and sailed on 10 January 1968 at 10.30 in the morning. *Jaguar* arrived at Portland on 22 January and remained there until arriving back at Chatham Dockyard on 13 March.

Whilst at Chatham Dockyard maintenance was carried out onboard the frigate. This was completed by the time she sailed for Portsmouth before taking part in April's *Exercise Dawn Patrol*. On Friday 26 April 1968 *Jaguar* took up station on *Britannia* for a photo opportunity. Later the frigate took part in *Exercise Dawn Patrol* on 29 April. The next month saw the frigate paying visits to Athens, Istanbul and on 25 May to Gibraltar. Gibraltar was left on 26 May and marked the end of her time in the Mediterranean. Four days later she arrived at Rosyth in time for 'Navy Days'. Following this she started preparations for her participation in *Exercise Orkex*, off Scapa Flow, which saw her operating with *Juno* and *Decoy*, the exercise lasted until 10 June around the Orkney Islands. On 14 June she arrived back at Portsmouth before undertaking a lengthy period of 'Sea Days'.

Jaguar left Portsmouth on July 20 and sailed north to take part in one of the largest naval exercises of the year. *Exercise Forthex* involved almost forty Royal Navy vessels. On 1 August she left the exercise area and returned to Portsmouth, where she arrived on 2 August. The next day she assumed the role of guardship at the annual Cowes week yacht festival on the Isle of Wight. On Tuesday 6 August *Jaguar* welcomed onboard a Royal Party, HRH Duke of Edinburgh was accompanied by his daughter, Princess Anne, Princess Alexandra and the Hon Angus Ogilvy who in turn were accompanied by C-in-C Portsmouth, Admiral Sir John Frewen. Two days later Princess Alexandra and Hon Angus Ogilvy made a return visit to the frigate. On the final day of Cowes week, *Jaguar* was in one of the best positions to see the fireworks display that lasted for forty-five minutes over Cowes. Following this public relations exercise, *Jaguar* returned home to Chatham Dockyard on 13 August.

On Sunday 1 September *Jaguar* was opened to the public for Chatham Navy Days and welcomed onboard thousands of local and international visitors over the two-day event. On Friday 6 September *Jaguar* left Chatham Dockyard for Devonport, where she arrived after a fast dash down the English Channel. After two days she slipped and after operating with other Royal Navy vessels, visited Amsterdam. This was followed by September's *Exercise Silver Tower*, which concluded with the frigate's arrival at Devonport on 25 September.

Upon her return to Chatham after another fast dash from Devonport, *Jaguar* entered a period of maintenance that continued until 16 October. Having left Chatham she arrived at Portsmouth on 18 October at the start of another deployment to the Mediterranean.

After two-day's spent at Gibraltar from 26 October *Jaguar* went on to visit the French resort of Marseilles at the end of the month. November saw the frigate at the French Naval Base at Toulon following joint manoeuvres with the French Navy, before both navies took part in *Exercise Eden Apple* for eleven days from 5 November. The beautiful Italian City of Naples was visited on 16 November, before *Jaguar* sailed onto Malta. She remained there until 27 November when she sailed for Gibraltar and onward journey back to Portsmouth. On 6 December *Jaguar* returned to Chatham and soon after was docked down for maintenance within the dockyard.

On 12 December command of the frigate was transferred to Commander M C Clapp. With most of the crew given shore leave during the festive period, the work on the frigate proceeded apace and upon the crew's return the ship returned to operational status on 10 January 1969, when she left dry dock.

20 January 1969 *Jaguar* sailed from Chatham and spent the remainder of the month conducting trials and working up off Portland and Portsmouth. She left the latter on 28 January to visit Culdrose in Cornwall and to operate with aircraft from the Royal Naval Air Station, HMS Seahawk. After this she sailed south from British waters to Gibraltar, whilst on passage to the Far East.

After seventeen days at sea, *Jaguar* arrived at Simonstown, where she stayed until 3 March. Four days later the frigate started a spell on Beira patrol, which ended on 28 March. *Jaguar* then sailed for a maintenance and leave period at Mombassa. The Beira patrol resumed on 18 April and would see the frigate remaining on station in the Mozambique Channel until 5 May. Three days later she arrived at the island of Coetivy in the Seychelles chain. Another tropical-island paradise, this time Trincomalee, was visited for two days from 13 May.

In May, the medical teams onboard *Jaguar* gave medical assistance to the people of the coral reef Island of Astore, in the Indian Ocean, after one of the islanders died from a case of tetanus. Later whilst operating with the frigate *Zulu*, *Jaguar* suffered a serious loss of her fresh water producing capacity. The *Zulu* was, however, capable of producing more than necessary and arranged to share it with *Jaguar*. The water transfer was through a fire hose slung on canvas stirrups from a light jackstay. The faulty equipment was repaired upon her arrival at Singapore on 19 May. After further maintenance, *Jaguar* sailed on 9 June to take in visits to Subic and a short Japanese tour visiting Yokohama and Muroran until late June 1969.

On 4 July she arrived at Hong Kong for repairs and maintenance, which were completed on 24 July. The next day the frigate slipped and sailed for Subic, where she would remain until the end of the month. After some days at sea, *Jaguar* arrived at Auckland on 12 August for *Exercise Longex* that would last for eleven days until 23 August. At the end of the exercise *Jaguar* arrived at Auckland. The frigate stayed overnight at the port before sailing to Dunedin where she remained until the end of the month.

September saw visits to Devonport in Tasmania, Port Kimbla and on 9 September Sydney for maintenance. The next port on the itinerary was Jervis Bay where she stayed alongside until 3 October. In October *Jaguar* went onto visit New Plymouth, Fiji, Tonga and the paradise-island of Tahiti. Many amongst the crew were saddened to leave this lovely island, but leave they did on 27 October.

Three days later *Jaguar* together with the tanker *Tidereach* visited Pitcairn Island at 09.00 hours to 19.00 hours. Some of the crew went ashore and accepted cool fruit drinks offered by the locals. The visit was only a short one, with the two ships leaving at 19.00 in the afternoon of 1 November. After a further eleven days at sea crossing the Pacific Ocean, the ship arrived at Balboa on 12 November. Later the same day she started her transit of the Panama Canal. *Jaguar* crossed from the Pacific to the Atlantic Ocean overnight and once in the Atlantic made her way to the US Navy Base, Key West. The welcome from the American's was as warm and friendly as ever and most of the crew accepted invitations to bars, clubs and barbecues from naval personnel stationed at Key West.

Jaguar left the US Navy base on 26 November and headed to the Jamaican Capital of Kingston. Just two days were spent there before she sailed for an appointment at San Juan and onto a homecoming at Portsmouth on 13 December. After three days alongside, *Jaguar* sailed for Chatham, where she arrived on 17 December. Whilst at Chatham she entered into a much needed refit, which started on 26 January 1970

Two days later saw another change of command ceremony when Commander L M N Saunders took the captain's chair for the first time. His time in command was to be brief as on 10 August 1970 command was again changed to Commander F A Collins. *Jaguar* completed her refit in late September, and commenced a period of trials. *Jaguar* re-commissioned at Chatham on October 17 1970. Present at the ceremony was Rear Admiral F C W Lawson, flag Officer Medway.

The rest of the year was spent conducting trials out of Chatham where Christmas was spent. On January 9 *Jaguar* sailed from Chatham Dockyard before spending some time at Portland. *Jaguar* spent the early part of February at Portsmouth undertaking a period of self maintenance, before joining other Royal Navy warships for that years annual exercise *Medtrain* on 18 February. After two days of exercises the frigate assumed the role of Gibraltar guardship. Having returned to Portsmouth on 11 March, *Jaguar* returned to Chatham Dockyard on 13 March for some maintenance and docking where she stayed for the next month.

After some time at Portland for weapons training, *Jaguar* sailed south to Gibraltar, arriving at the colony on 3 May. May saw further visits to Teneriffe and Tristan da Cunha before arriving at Gough Island.

The island had been discovered in the 16th century by the Portuguese navigator, Goncalo Alvarez. Then it was forgotten about until 1731 when Captain Gough of the ship *Richmond* re-sighted it and the island then became a location for British and American whalers. On March 28 1938, **HMS Milford** anchored off part of the island known as the

Glen and claimed the island for Britain and in so doing making it a dependency of St Helena. With no established port facilities *Jaguar* like the *Milford* anchored off the island and provided the scientists on the island who were monitoring weather conditions with food and checked on their medical needs. She left the island after four days and made for Simonstown, where the frigate arrived on 4 June.

Six days were spent alongside before *Jaguar* entered into the Indian Ocean and after calling at Gan for fuel, arrived at Singapore on 26 June. On 19 July she left and sailed south to Sydney in Australia to take part in the large-scale naval exercise *Southern Clime*. Before taking part the ship's crew enjoyed five days at Sydney, with many taking to the cities bars and clubs, while others just enjoyed the Southern Hemisphere's winter sunshine.

On Monday 9 August *Jaguar* started her duties as part of *Exercise Southern Clime*, the exercise was, however, cancelled due to bad weather. *Jaguar* later joined the aircraft carrier *Eagle* and the destroyer and frigates *Glamorgan, Danae, Achilles, HMAS Ovens, HMNZS Waikato* and *HMNZS Wirangi* and visited Wellington in New Zealand. On 20 August the frigate arrived at Dunedin for six-days.

On 3 September *Exercise Flyex* occupied the ship until 9 September. The previous day she had arrived at the port of Bunbury before conducting more exercises in local waters until 20 September. Two days later *Jaguar* was back at Singapore, where repairs and maintenance was carried out until 19 November. *Jaguar* had been assigned to ANZUK forces from the beginning of November until 2 December and during this time, visited Manila, before sailing onto Hong Kong, on 2 December.

On 6 December 1971 command of the frigate was yet again changed with Commander G W G Hunt taking command. Commander Hunt entered the Royal Navy in 1949 as a Naval Cadet at the Britannia Royal Naval College. In 1955 he became a naval pilot. Between 1958 and 1969 he served in the aircraft carriers *Albion, Hermes, Ark Royal* and *Eagle*. From 1962 to 1964 he was loaned to the United States Navy for instructional duties with a Phantom squadron. Upon his return he commanded 764, 766 and 899 squadrons before being promoted to Commander in 1969. A period of time was also spent at the Ministry of Defence before his appointment to command *Jaguar*.

Jaguar left Hong Kong on 13 December and visited Subic before returning to Hong Kong after nine days away. Christmas and New Year was spent at the colony before slipping out of port on 10 January 1972. Singapore was next on the agenda for the frigate, where she arrived after four days at sea. On 19 January *Jaguar* left to visit the tropical island of Gan, where she fuelled.

The frigate had just finished exercising off Pulau Aur Island in the China Sea and was preparing to collect a troop of Commando's from the beach when the troop-leader was approached, by a man and a boy called Abu Faman Abu Bakar. The boy had a bad tooth abscess and needed medical attention. A Malaysian apprentice serving in *Jaguar* Soon Tat Kong became translator. There followed a 100-mile dash to Singapore for dental treatment.

The early part of 1972 proved to be as exciting and diverse as any year in her career to date. On 3 February *Jaguar* represented the United Kingdom for the Ethiopian Navy Days, when she visited Massawa. The need for warships to enforce the oil embargo on the Beira Patrol meant that *Jaguar*, with her long range diesel engines was required in the area and after a twelve-day maintenance period at Mombassa, she arrived on station on 27 February. Her first patrol would last until 13 March, during which time she intercepted and inspected numerous merchant ships to ensure compliance with the oil embargo.

On St Patrick's Day 1972 *Jaguar* sailed into Simonstown and secured alongside, much to the relief of the crew, who were granted some time ashore. The frigate slipped on 24 March to start her long voyage up the West Coast of Africa to return home to the United Kingdom. She made no stops until 8 April, when she put into Gibraltar. Two days were spent there to allow the crew a chance to buy last minute gifts for loved one's back home and to refuel and restock the ships' supplies. On 13 April *Jaguar* sailed up the Solent and secured at Portsmouth.

After four days she sailed to Chatham, where *Jaguar* arrived at 15.30 on 18 April. After a period in dry dock, *Jaguar's* refit was completed on 21 May. The home leg of her commission started on 2 June when *Jaguar* sailed from Chatham. After visits to Portsmouth and Portland, the frigate was at Minehead on 24 June. After three days at the Devon holiday resort, she sailed to another holiday destination, this time Teignmouth, where she arrived on 28 June. Whilst there *Jaguar's* 'pirates' entertained a group of physically handicapped children.

Such fun was left behind on 6 July when *Jaguar* sailed to take part in the serious business of *Exercise West Ho* that was held between 7 and 18 July 1972. Six days later the ship sailed up the River Tamar to secure within Devonport dockyard. This proved to be a short two-day visit, before the frigate slipped to sail back to Chatham Dockyard, where she arrived on 21 July. Seasonal leave was granted to the crew, but many were onboard her during August when she was present at Chatham Navy Days.

Jaguar slipped from the base on 29 August to operate in the Mediterranean. Her first stop was at Gibraltar on 1 September. Whilst later in the month, she visited Malta and Tangiers. The beginning of October saw the frigate operating with the assault ship *Intrepid* again off Malta before calling at the Turkish seaside-city of Izmir on 11 October. During this visit, the Royal Navy ship gave assistance to a merchant ship.

The Lebanese *Beiteddine* had fouled her screw with a rope and asked the Royal Navy for help. *Jaguar's* diving officer, Sub Lieutenant Anthony Maher dived in complete darkness. He located the offending rope and cut it free. Two American divers from the *USS Barry* had assisted him.

The 'Jolly Jag' joined the *Barry*, the Turkish *Adatepe*, the Greek *Velos* and the Italian *Carabinierre* at Izmir to form a naval 'on call' force Mediterranean. The crews of the assembled ships all found time to enjoy the many and varied ashore attractions which ranged from Roman and Byzantine remains to belly dancers in night-clubs of nearby Ephesus.

On 15 October *Jaguar* left Izmir and two days later arrived at Kalamata, where the 'on call' force staged an international 'cook in', where the crews all tasted and sampled each other countries national and favourite food dishes.

Jaguar headed back across the Adriatic and called in at the Italian City of Trieste on 22 October, before continuing her journey home to Chatham via Portland. She arrived back at Chatham on 3 November. Whilst she was alongside in the Dockyard a drama occurred when a workman fell into the dock. Lieutenant Frank Newton, Marine Engineering Officer of the frigate dived into save the workman Frank Fordhan. Mr Fordhan, an elderly workman, had been painting the bogie of 914 crane on the west of Basin 3 when he lost his footing on the devilled coping-stones at the edge of the basin. Mr Fordhan fell on to the catamaran between *Jaguar* and the basin wall and rolled into the water. In his fall he broke his wrist, fractured a rib, severely bruised his thigh and suffered shock. Lieutenant Newton quickly dived into the water, fully clothed and pulled Mr Fordham to safety.

Jaguar returned to sea on 23 November to visit Rosyth the next day. Three days were spent at the Scottish Naval Base before the frigate slipped and headed down the Forth River.

On 29 November *Jaguar* started a fishery patrol, which lasted until 18 December. The next day the frigate secured within Chatham Dockyard. She remained there over Christmas and New Year. On 9 January 1973 she was at Portsmouth before returning to Chatham for a brief docking period. Commander Bellingham took command of the ship on 15 February and took her out to sea a week later. On 23 February as she arrived at Portsmouth, *Jaguar* had an unfortunate accident, when *Jaguar* was coming alongside the frigate *Grenville* moored at North Corner Jetty when she crashed into the older frigate. A Navy spokesman said, "*Jaguar's* bow's were badly crumpled. The other ship had a gash in the side. Diver's are preparing a report on the extent of the underwater damage."

No one was hurt but it took three tugs to wrench the two warships apart. *Jaguar* was out of action for a number of weeks during which time the damage was repaired. When she returned to duty and after working up at Portland, the frigate sailed south for

Gibraltar, where she arrived on 2 April. *Jaguar* visited the Portuguese Capital City of Lisbon between 30 April and 4 May, before returning to Gibraltar. She remained there for the next ten days before sailing for a visit to Port Vendres two days later.

Five days were spent there before again returning to Gibraltar and the return trip to the United Kingdom. *Jaguar* arrived at Rosyth on 28 May. The need for frigates to patrol Icelandic fishery areas meant that *Jaguar* was need on the front line of the so-called 'Cod War'. After two days at Rosyth she started a fishery patrol off Iceland. During this patrol, there was a near miss with the Icelandic gunboat *Aegir*, when the gunboat almost struck the Royal Navy frigate on 10 June. After a six-day visit to the Norwegian port of Trondheim on 19 June, *Jaguar* sailed south and arrived back at Chatham Dockyard on 28 June.

Maintenance and leave was carried out in the summer months and only on 6 August 1973 did *Jaguar* leave Chatham Dockyard at 09.20 in the morning. The next day she arrived at Portsmouth for a period of weapons training and to operate as the guardship for that year's Fastnet Yacht race, held between 11 and 17 August.

During the races *Jaguar* became involved in two emergencies, which both turned out to be false alarms. The *Jaguar* organised a search following a message that a yacht was sinking twenty miles south of Portland Bill. The other incident occurred later and was off the Cornish coast when the *Jaguar* sped in thick haze to what appeared to be a yacht on fire but proved to be a flare dropped by a Sea King helicopter from RNAS Culdrose.

On 18 August *Jaguar* arrived at Devonport before visiting Portsmouth and Rosyth towards the end of the month. On 29 August she left the Scottish Naval Base to start another stint off Iceland. On September 10, the Icelandic gunboat *Thor* rammed *Jaguar*. Two days later the frigate was relieved and ordered back to Rosyth, where the damage inflicted by the *Thor*, could be inspected. *Jaguar* left Rosyth on 17 September to have the damage repaired at Chatham Dockyard, where she arrived the following day.

After repairs had been made, *Jaguar* again headed off to Icelandic waters in October 1973. After a brief stop at Rosyth on 7 October, she commenced her patrol on 10

October. This patrol was however, without any incident unlike the last patrol and was completed on 1 November.

Four days later *Jaguar* arrived at Portsmouth for a four-day rest period for the crew. When she left on the 9 November, *Jaguar* crossed the English Channel for a four-day visit to the Channel Island of Guernsey. On her return crossing the crew prepared the ship's paying off pennant and as she entered the Solent, the pennant was streamed. She arrived at Portsmouth on 13 November. Five days later *Jaguar* slipped and headed back to sea for the short voyage to Chatham Dockyard, where she arrived at 09.35 on 20 November. She entered the Dockyard through the North Lock. On 3 December 1973 *Jaguar* started a short refit, which prepared her for the standby squadron within the dockyard to await her next call to arms.

Jaguar spent the next two years in the standby squadron until 1976 when she re-commissioned for service off Iceland. On 30 January *Jaguar* left Chatham Dockyard and spent the next weeks conducting trials in and around Chatham and at sea until 19 March when she returned to base.

On 27 May 1976 *Jaguar's* final commanding officer, Commander D I Rhodes joined the warship. On 11 June 1976 she left Chatham Dockyard for a further spell of trials. After some gruelling times in the North Atlantic the frigate returned to Chatham Dockyard on 9 July 1976. It was to be a relatively short visit, when on 26 July she slipped out for another patrol, which lasted until 23 August when she once more returned to Chatham. *Jaguar* remained in the port until 24 September.

The Cod War of 1976 for which, *Jaguar* was re-commissioned, came to an end towards the end of the year and before *Jaguar* had been fully worked up. The ship had been fitted with heavy wooden sheathing on the bow and stern plus extra internal shoring to protect the ship from the dangerous manoeuvres undertaken by Icelandic gunboats. The frigate did not make any fishery patrols and only remained in commission for six months before returning to the Standby Squadron at Chatham Dockyard.

1977 and the first seven months of 1978 were spent in reserve, until a delegation from the Bangladeshi Navy expressed an interest in purchasing the frigate. The Royal

Navy assisted in the sale and on 16 July 1978 she was sold and was renamed *Ali Haider* in a ceremony held at Chatham. The frigate left Chatham for the last time as the *Ali Haider* on 16 October 1978. *Ali Haider* was taken to Southampton to be refitted by Vosper Thornycroft where the work was undertaken between August and October 1978.

In Bangladeshi service the ship has served as a principal naval unit and as a training vessel for generations of naval staff. After many years of useful service *Ali Haider* paid off in 2001

PUMA

Puma was ordered from the Glasgow yard of Scotts and was subsequently laid down on the morning of 16 November 1953. Construction work on the frigate continued at a steady pace until she was launched with all due and customary ceremony on 30 June 1954. To finish the frigate took a couple of more years but all work on *Puma* was completed on 27 April 1957.

After the shipbuilder's had carried out builder's trials it was the turn of the Royal Navy who chose the summer in which to carry out these tests in the waters around the Isle of Arran and the Clyde approaches. Having been accepted into service the Royal Navy's latest frigate's, first deployment would further re-enforce the belief in the long legs of the diesel-powered frigates. *Puma* was heading south.

First port of call was on 15 September when *Puma* arrived at Freetown. Five days of exchange visits followed, which allowed many amongst the frigate's crew to explore the town and further afield, although most of the crew soon discovered just how poor the local population was. After five days the frigate slipped back down river and headed back out into the Atlantic Ocean. Next port of call was to Santa Cruz on Teneriffe for a brief two-day stay. On 30 September she arrived back at Plymouth and soon there after travelled the short distance to Portsmouth. The remainder of 1957 was spent on trials and exercises before returning to Plymouth for a docking period that started on 27 January 1958. On St Patrick's Day 1958 Commander Richard Pilkington Clayton assumed command. He started his career as a midshipman on the cruiser *Cumberland* between 1942 and 1943. The following year he moved to the Home Fleet destroyers where he stayed until 1946. His next appointment was to the destroyer *Comus* in the Far East. Four years were spent in the Training Squadron Destroyers until 1953. Three years later during the Suez Crisis Richard Clayton was serving onboard *Striker*. 1957 was spent at the Staff College before assuming command of *Puma*.

After his time in *Puma*, he became executive officer of the cruiser *Lion* and took command of the destroyers *Kent* and *Hampshire*. Between 1976 and 1979 he was

Controller of the Navy and the Third Sea Lord. 1979 saw a promotion to Commander in Chief, Naval Home Command until 1981.

Puma remained in the docks at Plymouth until 11 April and conducted trials over the next few weeks. On 26 April *Puma* arrived at Portland and stayed in the area for the next month and a half fine tuning the equipment and men. At the beginning of June she returned briefly to Plymouth before starting her first tour of duty on the South African and South Atlantic Station, based at Simonstown. *Puma* arrived at Simonstown on 26 June, with stop over's at Freetown and Monrovia.

After only two days at Simonstown, *Puma* left the naval base and sailed for Durban. After eleven days alongside, during which the crew enjoyed many social and sporting events, the frigate sailed on to her next destination at Majunga, during the passage she sailed with the frigate *Bigbury Bay*. Majunga was reached on 18 July and again many firm friendships were cultivated during the three-day visit. *Puma's* crew, were enjoying the warm sunshine in the Indian Ocean throughout July and went onto visit Lourenco Marques, Penm and Kamaran, before sailing into Aden on 2 August.

Later in the month on 31 August the frigate arrived at Karachi and exercised with local naval forces in the area. The following month, however, *Puma* became involved in one of the decade's most celebrated maritime salvage operations.

Puma was operating with the aircraft carrier *Bulwark* in the Persian Gulf on 12 September when two tankers, the Liberian *Melika* and the French *Fernand Gilabert*, collided in the Gulf of Oman and caught fire. "One of the finest salvage operations of recent times" was how the Admiralty described the work.

The aircraft carrier *Bulwark*, together with her escorts was around 130 miles away when at 07.00 the SOS was received from the two ships. *Bulwark, Loch Killisport, Puma* and *St Bride's Bay* made for the scene of the accident, along with a number of merchant ships.

When the Royal Navy ships arrived on the scene, they found the *Melika* ablaze amidships and rolling considerably. After some time a line was secured and the *Bulwark* took the tanker under tow. After two hours the strain broke the towline and a second had to be secured and this time the *Puma* secured a second line to the stern of the tanker to act as a rudder. At Muscat *Bulwark* was relieved by the cruiser *Sheffield* and the oil from the *Melika*, was transferred to other tankers.

Following this success *Puma* paid a visit to Bahrain, which was left on 21 October as the frigate started to retrace her course back to her South African base. After a brief call at Aden, the frigate continued south and arrived at Mombassa on 7 November.

Three days later *Puma* arrived at Port Victoria in the beautiful and serene surroundings of the Seychelles. Four days were spent in these magnificent islands just feet above the water in the middle of the Indian Ocean. The crystal blue waters and excellent fishing around these small islands was fully taken advantage of by the frigate's crew. With much sadness the ship and crew left the Seychelles and started off for the equally exotic destination of Port Louis on the island of Mauritius. Being a much larger island more time had been arranged on *Puma's* schedule and eventually eleven days were spent at Port Louis.

By the time *Puma* had returned to Simonstown she was in need of a period of self-maintenance. This was followed up by a further period in dock, which was completed on 31 January 1959. On 2 February she left and headed for Saldanha, where she arrived the following morning. Seventeen days later she slipped and returned to Simonstown.

Another period of self-maintenance followed, which was completed at the end of February. March was a busy month for *Puma* with visits to Lagos and St Helena before sailing back into Simonstown navy base on 26 March 1959.

April would see *Puma* cross the Atlantic and visit South America. Her first port visit was on 27 April when she arrived at Santos. Five days were spent exploring the town and countryside before making her way to her next destination of Salvador. On 11 May she left and made the short journey to Recife. After four days she left and crossed to Pointe a Pierre on the island of Trinidad. Ponta Delgada was next on the agenda after an Atlantic crossing. Finally, on 9 June 1959 the British summer weather welcomed the frigate back to Plymouth. After the crew, were granted leave, *Puma* was taken in hand for a refit within Devonport Dockyard.

Puma's next commanding officer, Commander J Marriott joined the ship on 18 August and oversaw the final stages of the frigate's refit, which was completed towards the end of October 1959. Following trials *Puma* arrived at Portland on 9 November 1959 for work ups. December saw port visits to Portland and Milford Haven before a return to Devonport on 12 December when Christmas leave was granted to the crew.

1960 started with a visit to Portsmouth, before starting her journey south via Gibraltar. On 5 February *Puma* arrived at the holiday destination of Las Palmas, although vacations were far from the minds of the crew as the ship was put through its paces. After three days, with some time spent ashore for the crew the frigate continued her voyage. Before arriving at Conakry on 19 February, *Puma* had paid brief visits to Dakar and Bathurst. Conakry was followed by Freetown and Monrovia before she arrived at Abidjan on 3 March 1960. *Puma's* tour of the smaller but still very important ports on the African West Coast continued throughout the early days of March with visits to Lagos, Port Harcourt, Takoradi, Tema, Pointe Noire, Banana and Lyanda before finally sailing into the large port at Simonstown on 4 April.

Essential maintenance was carried out with the assistance of some dockyard workers over the next fortnight before slipping out of port on 17 May. *Puma* headed out to sea for three days to operate in the Saldanka region before returning to base.

On 25 May *Puma* departed Simonstown for a short visit to East London, before again returning to Simonstown. *Puma* continued to operate in this pattern for most of the summer months, before slipping on 12 August to start a crossing of the Atlantic and visit the countries of South America. First country to receive a port of call was Uruguay, when the British frigate sedately entered the port of Montevideo on 23 August. Those amongst the crew who had hoped to see the city were in for a disappointment as *Puma* only spent a few hours there, replenishing her fuel and supplies before sailing for Buenos Aires in Argentina, where she arrived the following day. In the Argentine capital, the crew, were not to be disappointed by what they found. With the ship staying in the port area of the city there was plenty of opportunity to explore the cultural delights of the region in addition to the large number of café's and bars. After eight very enjoyable days alongside *Puma* slipped away from the quayside and sailed for her next appointment at Santos on 4

September. At Santos, the Royal Navy was given the honour of leading a parade to mark the 138th anniversary of Brazilian independence.

A ceremonial guard from *Puma* led the parade of 5000 troops with the march past taking 45 minutes to complete. To reciprocate the compliment, *Puma* sailed on the 7 September under the orders of the Brazilian destroyer *Marcilio Diaz* for exercises whilst en route to Rio de Janeiro, where she arrived on the morning of 8 September to glorious sunshine. Another opportunity to soak up the culture of South America was on offer during the nine days spent in Brazil's most exotic city. A great many of the crew took bus trips to see the monument of Christ that dominates the mountains behind the city, whilst those who wished to rest decided to laze on the wide golden sandy beaches and warm seas.

Finally on 17 September the frigate left and started her return crossing of the South Atlantic and headed for Port Harcourt. At Ascension Island the ship stayed for just ten hours before continuing her journey. After eleven days at sea, it was with some relief that land was sighted and within hours *Puma* had secured alongside. As part of her visit, *Puma* represented the British government at the Nigerian Independence Day Celebrations and a contingent of men from the frigate marched through the main town. After six days rest and leave *Puma* slipped out of port. Four days out of port on 8 October the ship went to emergency stations when a fire was discovered in the stabiliser room. It was quickly extinguished, but the cause was later discovered to be deliberate sabotage by James Sorley, a rating onboard the frigate. He was arrested and upon the ship's return to Simonstown on 12 October was taken off the ship to be punished. Before her arrival at Simonstown, however, the frigate participated in *CAPEX* off Luanda in Angola, where she operated with South African and Portuguese warships. Whilst not taking part in exercises the crew tried their hand at fishing. The waters around Luanda are infested with sharks and at one time five were seen in a cluster. The shark hook was streamed and Bren guns opened fire but no luck in catching any.

A ten-day maintenance period was started upon the frigate's return to Simonstown, which also saw a Captain F (7) inspection. On 14 November *Puma* left Simonstown at the start of the second phase of the *CAPEX* exercises, this was followed by a short visit to Port Elizabeth and a return to Simonstown. *Puma's* return trip to the United Kingdom started on 28 November when she slipped out of Simonstown and made for the desolate and isolated island of St Helena in the middle of the Atlantic Ocean. The islanders there greeted the ship and her crew enthusiastically and welcomed them onto the island. In exchange, the ship's medical team made sure everyone on the island was in good health and also landed much needed supplies for the islanders. *Puma* arrived and left on the same day, 3 December. Freetown in Sierra Leone was her next destination, where the frigate restocked her supplies and fuelled. She remained alongside only long enough to complete these tasks before commencing her northward journey once more. Gibraltar was reached on 14 December, where the crew, were given two days in which to obtain any last items for family and friends. She slipped on the morning of 16 December and arrived at Devonport three days later. As she pulled into her berth at Devonport a live puma called Flora from Paignton zoo was on the quayside to greet the ship of the same name.

Puma, was taken in hand for an extensive refit and reconditioning of all her equipment and machinery, which lasted until mid February 1961. She shuttled between Devonport, Portsmouth, Spithead and Portland over the next few months carrying out post refit trials before being declared operational to the fleet at the beginning of March 1961.

On 3 March *Puma* left Portland and arrived at Devonport the same day. Five days later, with the growing dispute over fishery rights in the waters around Iceland, *Puma* was sent to the disputed waters and she slipped from Devonport on 8 March. She arrived on station after four days at sea and remained there until the final day of the month. Four days later she arrived back at Plymouth and after passing the historic breakwater she secured within the dockyard. Easter leave was granted to a very tired crew and after spending some much needed time with their families, they returned days before the ship left the dockyard on 4 May to take part in *JSC 115* off Londonderry.

After a two day visit to the Scilley Isles, *Puma* took part in *Exercise Cottage Window* until 31 May 1961. This was followed by *Exercise Shop Window* until 9 June. Two days later *Puma's* crew started the third exercise in two months. *Exercise Fairwind VI* started on 11 June and was carried out in the North Sea until 22 June. On that day the ship secured alongside at No 1 jetty at Aarhus. After four days rest and leave, the frigate sailed to Copenhagen with the cruiser *Bermuda* and the frigate *Undaunted*. Before arriving at the port, the assembled ships from many nations rendezvoused with the Danish Royal Yacht *Danneborg*, which led the other ships into port.

As is customary for Navy visits to foreign Countries trips were organised to take those who wished to visit the Carlsberg and Tuborg breweries. These free trips were very busy indeed.

Puma left Copenhagen with *Blackwood* on 2 July to sail south to the Baltic to visit Gdynia in Poland. As the ship berthed alongside a large naval guard and a band welcomed her. Also there to greet the frigate was a large number of civilians. The Polish Naval commander toured the ship. Next day the Captain, accompanied by twenty officers went by air to Warsaw. During her time at Gdynia *Puma* was thrown open to visitors, and in all 1,500 toured the frigate. *Puma* left on the afternoon of 6 July and set sail for the crossing to Londonderry, where she arrived after four days at sea.

After some training in Northern Ireland waters, *Puma* returned to Portsmouth on 4 August. After four days she sailed again, this time for Devonport to commence a refit. Captain D B N Mellis DSC joined the ship on 16 August 1961. *Puma's* commission ended on August 22 1961.

Puma's completed her refit on 15 December 1961 and after post refit trials the frigate carried out the usual few months worth of work-up's before starting her next deployment, which started in mid April 1962.

On the voyage south, *Puma* visited Gibraltar and Freetown before calling on Simonstown. July saw visits paid to Durban, Diego Suarez and Reunion Island, before returning to Simonstown on 28 July. The next month was spent conducting alongside maintenance, before sailing again on 27 September. On 2 October *Puma* visited the island of Tristan da Cunha in mid Atlantic for four days before returning to South Africa with a visit to Capetown on 11 October. On Wednesday 3 October she sustained damage to her Port propeller at 12.57 when the frigate struck an underwater object. In the captain's report on the incident, he stated that.

"On Tuesday 2nd October the ship was at anchor off the settlement at Tristan da Cunha in 14 fathoms, position 354 degrees E, W/T Mast 3.4 cables when I decided to rig a jackstay to the cliffs in order to transfer stores and demolition equipment to enable a landing party to effect an improvement to the access from the settlement to the new beach. To provide the necessary tension the off shore end of the rig had to be handled onboard."

The Captain went ashore at 10.45 with Mr Stableford, the island's administrator in the Islanders boat and returned onboard after a short tour of inspection at 12.35. All stores had been transferred and the rig disassembled. Twenty minutes later a series of soft bumps were felt, followed at 12.57 by a large bang when *Puma* struck the underwater object. The island of St Helena was next on the agenda with a planned visit to check on the health and welfare of the islanders and a similar visit to Ascension on 24 October. *Puma* arrived at Freetown on 28 October, before calling at Bathurst for a three-day visit on 1 November. Gibraltar was reached eight days later where further repairs were undertaken, these were completed on 28 November and *Puma* sailed south and

151

returned to Freetown for a two-day stopover, en route to Ascension Island.

Finally, *Puma* returned to Simonstown on 18 December 1962.

After celebrating Christmas at Simonstown, **Puma** left port on 8 January 1963 for exercises that would take her to Saldanha on 12 July. The port is South Africa's largest natural anchorage and deepest water and is only 60 miles from Cape Town. She remained in port overnight before sailing back to Simonstown the next morning.

On 23 January she left Simonstown with the frigate *Whitby* and headed to Mossel Bay and Port Elizabeth before returning to Simonstown on 29 January. The South American leg of the deployment started on 11 February when *Puma* slipped her moorings and headed out to sea to cross the South Atlantic to visit South America. In the coming months the frigate paid courtesy and official visits to Buenos Aires, Fray Bentos, Rio de Janeiro and after an Atlantic crossing, Las Palmas before finally arriving back home at Devonport on 1 April 1963.

In May **Puma** entered dry dock at Portsmouth Dockyard for an extended refit. On 6 January 1964 command of **Puma** transferred to Lt Commander P Harries. Later during the refit, the commanding officer, who would take the frigate back to sea took over command. He was Captain Martin Noel Lucey, DSC who took command from the Lt Commander on 4 May. Captain Lucey had joined the Royal Navy in 1938. As a sub lieutenant he was the navigating officer of the 2nd Escort Group in HMS *Douglas* and was later the 1st lieutenant of *Atherstone* during the Sicily and Salerno landings. He was awarded the DSC for actions against enemy coastal convoys in the Bay of Biscay whilst serving in the destroyer *Tartar*.

Later on 1 June a small fire broke out onboard but caused insignificant damage. In the closing stages of her extended refit, on 11 June 1964 **Puma** was subjected to a much larger and more substantial engine room fire. This fire came as the frigate was being prepared for the start of her trials and the damage caused the completion date of the refit to slip somewhat.

On 30 October 1964 *Puma* was finally re-commissioned with 7th FS at Portsmouth for service in the South Atlantic. The ship's company held a dance at HMS Excellent. The commissioning cake, which had been baked for the original pre fire commissioning was reused, but had to have a fresh layer of icing applied. Post refit trials and shakedown's continued throughout the winter months and were principally carried out in the waters around Portland, although there were a number of port visits in the United Kingdom and on the Continent to break the cycle for the crew. Furthermore, Christmas leave was taken and upon the crew's return *Puma* was brought up to fully operational status at Portsmouth on 5 February 1965.

1965 it was decided would be a year when the Royal Navy made a special effort to get seen by the general public and as a result commenced a large 'Meet the Royal Navy tour' of major and minor ports around the British Isles. *Puma* was detailed to be the ship that would conduct the tour that started in Dundee in June. *Puma* went onto to visit Aberdeen, The Moray Firth and the Kyle of Lochalsh before visiting Mallaig and Fort William. On 19 June 1965 *Puma* arrived at Oban and after welcoming onboard many locals left the next day. The policy of the Royal Navy was to visit as many ports as possible, this meant that except for the largest ports, *Puma* only stayed for a few hours at each location before sailing onto her next destination.

On 21 June *Puma* arrived at Ayr and left later the same day for Greenock, where she spent five days alongside and welcomed onboard many thousands of local people. On 28 June it was the turn of Wales to receive *Puma*, when she arrived at Llandudno. The frigate went onto visit Holyhead before sailing for a maintenance period at Plymouth on 5 July. On 12 July she resumed her 'Meet the Royal Navy' tour, with a hugely successful visit to Liverpool. Many thousands came to visit the frigate and learn about a life in the Royal Navy. On 20 July *Puma* slipped from the Liverpool dockside and instead of sailing into the Irish Sea she sailed up the River Mersey and entered the Manchester Ship Canal for a visit to Britain's largest inland port city. She arrived on 21 July and secured within the dock complex. Four days were spent in Manchester and yet again, thousands of people came to view the ship and talk to her crew.

After exiting into the Irish Sea, it was off to Loch Ewe on 27 July for a three-day visit. On 31 July *Puma* arrived back at Plymouth and spent a few weeks alongside before sailing to the Clyde, where she arrived on 8 August.

Monday 9 August found the frigate anchored in the River Clyde with no wind and the Firth of Clyde a glassy calm. *Puma* was one of fifty ships present to be reviewed by Her Majesty Queen Elizabeth II in the Royal Yacht *Britannia*. The following morning the frigate left and started preparations for Exercise 'Rock Haul', which lasted until 23 August, when the frigate arrived at Cardiff. After two days at the Welsh Capital City *Puma* sailed to visit Swansea. On 29 August it was Torbay's turn to receive the frigate and as elsewhere *Puma* was inundated with curious members of the public asking many questions of the crew about life in the Royal Navy. The Meet the Royal Navy Tour continued throughout the summer and into autumn 1965, with visits to most of the major seaports around the British coastline, plus Guernsey in the Channel Islands and anchoring off Lyme Regis on September 9.

On 13 September 1965 *Puma* arrived at Portsmouth and stayed until 11 October when she slipped from Portsmouth and sailed the short distance to Portland. Crew training took up the whole of October and was spread between Portland, Penzance and Devonport, where she arrived on 22 October. Three days later she sailed for Londonderry area.

The training period, in the Irish Sea was intense but at its completion the crew, were pleased to be allowed Christmas leave after the ship had docked at Devonport. After a maintenance period *Puma* sailed from Devonport on 3 January 1966 for the South African and South Atlantic station.

After calling at Gibraltar, *Puma* called at Port Etienne almost a week later for a two-day port of call. Amongst the interesting ports visited during the passage south to Simonstown were Dakar, Takoradi, Lagos, Lome and Abidjan. On 14 February the frigate arrived at Bathurst and spent seven days in port, which allowed members of her crew to explore the local countryside. After leaving Bathurst on 21 February *Puma* visited Monrovia, Buchannan, Ascension Island, St Helena and Tristan da Cunha. At the island the frigate's crew were tasked with assessing the possibility of rehabilitating the island after the volcanic eruption. Amongst many tasks ashore was the construction of a road from the only serviceable beach on the island. Numerous rocks were blasted to make way for what was christened Puma Road. *Puma* arrived on 23 March at Simonstown. *Puma* undertook a maintenance period, which lasted until 5 April. Two days later she slipped out to sea and started her first patrol on the Beira Patrol, designed to prevent oil being transported to Rhodesia. *Puma's* patrol started on 11 April and involved sailing up and down in the Mozambique Channel, challenging and inspecting any vessel suspected of smuggling oil.

On 12 April 1966 Captain C J Cunningham took command of the frigate. Captain Cunningham joined the Royal Navy by Direct Entry from the Nautical College, Pangbourne in January 1939. During the war he served in the Atlantic, Norway, the Mediterranean, the Far East and in the Russian Convoys.

Following her time on oil embargo patrol, *Puma* sailed into Simonstown on 25 April to allow her crew a few days leave. Two days later she sailed to Tamatave for a two-day visit. After this visit the frigate visited Diego Suarez, Port Louis on the island of Mauritius and St Denis on Reunion Island before returning to Simonstown on 26 May 1966.

The ship took part in a series of exercises with the South African Navy in the Simonstown area in early June. *Puma's* second tour of duty on the Beira Patrol started on 8 July and saw her operating in the Mozambique Channel until 14 July. A couple of months for maintenance and leave followed her return to Simonstown.

On 9 August 1966 *Puma* left to resume the patrols in the Mozambique Channel between 30 August and 2 September. September, however, brought a change of scenery. *Puma* was ordered to sail to Falkland Islands 'as a precautionary measure' to take off 20 'pirates' from the 'Condor' movement who had seized an Argentine DC4 aeroplane and landed at Port Stanley racecourse with the idea of starting an invasion.

During the flurry of diplomatic communication that ensued, Britain proposed to Argentina, who did not endorse the endeavour that they should send a ship to repatriate their 'citizens' from the Falklands. Argentina counter proposed that *Puma* could take the twenty back to the mainland.

The 'invasion' never amounted to much more than a political problem of repatriating the nineteen young men and one young blonde woman. After one blunt refusal to surrender, they did indeed surrender to the local Roman Catholic priest, Father Rodolfo Roel. They were arrested and held under guard at Port Stanley's St Mary's Catholic Church annexe. The other twenty-six passengers and crew of the airliner left the islands in the Royal Mail ship *Darwin.*

Once the situation on the Falklands had been resolved peacefully, *Puma* resumed her planned schedule with visits to Tristan da Cunha and Continental South America. Each of the planned port visits took her progressively north, Puerto Belgrano was first stop, then Montevideo, Rio de Janeiro and on 18 November *Puma* arrived for a four-day visit to Salvador. After more visits in the region, *Puma* returned home to the United Kingdom and soon was in dockyard hands once again for a long refit that would see her out of action until the beginning of June 1967.

After an extensive rectification program, *Puma* next ventured to sea on 5 August 1967 and made for Portland. After three days conducting trials, the frigate secured at Devonport and spent the best part of August in the base, including being open to the public during Navy Days held over the late August Bank Holiday weekend. She slipped out of port on 29 August and returned to Portland.

Puma remained in and around Portland for most of the autumn and only sailed back into Portsmouth on 10 November. This visit was only to be for a few hours, as she sailed soon after crossing the English Channel and arrived at Jersey later the same day. Four days were spent on the Channel Island and the local inhabitants were given the opportunity of seeing one of the Royal Navy's frigates up close and personal. Being in such close proximity to the French coastline, the planned schedule had included a port visit to L'Orient on the 15 November and another successful port of call was recorded in the ships' log.

Upon leaving on 17 November *Puma's* crew commenced preparations for her active participation in *Exercise Midsummer* held over seven days from 18 November. At its conclusion, the frigate passed Plymouth breakwater and passed the Narrows to secure alongside at Devonport Dockyard. On 27 November, *Puma* was manoeuvred into No 27 dock in the dockyard to receive essential maintenance. On 6 December 1967 Commander J F H C de Winton assumed command. *Puma*, however, remained high and dry until 24 January 1968.

On 7 February *Puma* sailed from Devonport for Gibraltar her destination was South Africa and a return to the Beira Patrol that was still enforcing the oil embargo on Rhodesia. After a nine-day visit to Freetown, *Puma* arrived at Simonstown on 27 February.

Her first patrol of this deployment commenced on 7 March. After ten days of patrol, she was taken off the patrol for four days leave, which was taken at Majunga. On 21 March she resumed her Beira patrol, this time until 11 April. *Puma's* planned maintenance was to be undertaken at Singapore Dockyard and upon completion of her Beira patrol duties, she sailed across the Indian Ocean and arrived there on 23 April. *Puma* remained at Singapore until 28 June. Exercises at Subic with the US Navy and Australian Navy started on 1 July and continued until she left two days later, when she slipped from her consorts and made her way to Hong Kong. Hong Kong was always a preferred destination for Royal Navy sailors, with a myriad of exotic locations, bars and shore accommodation and during this visit, *Puma's* crew made full use of all the facilities available. On 12 July she sailed from Hong Kong to visit Bangkok three days later. After five-days spent in the city, ship and crew departed to sail to Singapore. July gave way to August and after a spell of self-maintenance *Puma* returned to the delights of Hong Kong from 15 August. She would remain in the province until 14 September

On Monday 16 September the aircraft carriers *Hermes* and *Bulwark* rendezvoused with *Puma, Glamorgan, Diana, Defender, Caprice, Forth Euraylus, Grenville* and *Parramatta* and the submarines *Cachalot* and *Andrew* for *Exercise Coral Seas* in the South China Sea. Later they joined forces with an amphibious force of *Albion, Intrepid, Triumph, Caprice* and *RFA Tidespring*. On 30 September *Puma* was off the coast of the Admiralty Islands for *Exercise 'Shadow'*. On Sunday 13 October 1968 the exercise finished and the Royal Navy force sailed to Sydney for a few days. *Puma* went onto visit Newcastle until 21 October. The rest of October was spent touring the many exotic South Sea Islands, such as Suva, Rotuna and at Fiji. Forty members of the crew led by the captain received the traditional Fijian welcome of the presentation of a whale's tooth and the exchanged of gifts, drinking kava and singing and dancing. After Fiji she sailed onto Funafuti. After Funafuti, was the long sea crossing to Pearl Harbor, which was reached on 6 November.

As per usual, the welcome from the United States Navy was amazing and many American sailors took their British colleagues on sight seeing tours of the main islands and even gave one or two lessons in surfboarding. After just three days in Hawaii, *Puma* left to continue her journey across the Pacific Ocean. Next landfall was San Francisco on California's West Coast. As *Puma* passed under the Golden Gate Bridge, the crew knew that the next four days in the City on the Bay was going to amongst the best of the deployment. Visits were laid onto all the cities main attractions.

The visit came to an end on 18 November when *Puma* once again sailed under the impressive Golden Gate Bridge and on into the Pacific Ocean, bound for the Panama Canal and the transit into the Atlantic Ocean. She arrived at Balboa after a short visit to Manzanillo on 28 November and transited the Panama Canal. On 29 November she visited Bluefields, before calling at Kingston on 2 December. Three days were spent at Kingston before *Puma* left for San Juan and Porto Delgada. From Porto Delgada it was only a relatively short trip back to Devonport, where the frigate arrived on 19 December.

1969 started with *Puma* in dockyard hands at Devonport, correcting all the many defects that had occurred since the frigate's last overhaul. The essential defects were all repaired by 31 January 1969 and after trials locally *Puma* left Devonport on 10 February.

Her first port of call was to Rothesay on 11 February to carry out submarine target exercises with the submarines from nearby Faslane. Indeed it was to Faslane that *Puma* sailed on 15 February. *Puma* continued to operate in the Rothesay area until late February, when she arrived back at Devonport on 24 February. The sunshine of Gibraltar was

Puma's next destination and her task there was to act as Guardship for the Rock until 21 March.

Having returned to Plymouth for some maintenance, *Puma* returned to Gibraltar to continue guardship duties until 9 May. Three days later the frigate paid a return visit to Jersey in the Channel Islands, before crossing the English Channel in order to take part the NATO review off Spithead. Twelve NATO countries sent warships to the Solent to celebrate twenty years of the North Atlantic Treaty Organisation and *Puma* was one of the sixty-three warships present to be reviewed by Her Majesty Queen Elizabeth II. Other Royal Navy ships present included the cruiser *Blake*, the destroyer *Glamorgan*. The US Navy was represented by a large number of warships centred on the aircraft carrier *USS Wasp* and *USS Dewey*. The Italian Navy's cruiser *Doria* and *De Alpino*, the Danish minelayer *Moen* and the Dutch cruiser *De Ruyter* were also present.

The HM Queen was in *Britannia*, was accompanied by the Duke of Edinburgh. The Secretary General of NATO, Signor Manilo Brosio, together with the Permanent Representatives to the North Atlantic Council, the Military Representatives of the NATO Military Committee and the major NATO Commanders were all there also.

Following the review, *Puma* received some maintenance at Portsmouth Dockyard before starting a period of shuttling between there and Portland throughout the early days of June. On 21 June *Puma* visited Kiel for an official visit to the German port. Seven days were spent there, which included the almost customary trip to the local breweries. The frigate sailed on 28 June and commenced refit upon her return to Devonport Dockyard on 30 June.

Commander A M G Pearson joined the ship as her commanding officer on 8 July 1969, but it would be almost a year until he could take her to sea. *Puma's* refit was completed in June 1970. After trials in and around Plymouth, the trials program moved to Portland in mid June 1970. On 19 June *Puma* was at Plymouth and declared operational from 25 June.

On 18 August she arrived at Shanklin on the Isle of Wight, but left after a few days to take part in *Exercise Rockhaul* until 12 September 1970. During the exercise the warship had visited Gibraltar and Tangiers. Two days after the end of the Exercise *Puma* arrived at Rapallo. This was followed by a very pleasant visit to the French port of Marseilles, where the Royal Navy ship was guest of the French Navy. Sporting challenges were set and the spoils were evenly split. *Puma* sailed on 23 September for Gibraltar and the start of her return to the United Kingdom. She arrived at Devonport on 29 September.

She next set sail on 9 November 1970 with *Salisbury* and arrived at Gibraltar six days later. Both ships were heading for the Far East and with the Suez Canal firmly closed the route chosen for the ships was via the Cape. Both ships arrived at Simonstown Dockyard on 2 December. *Puma* returned to Beira Patrol duties from 12 December. Christmas and New Year was spent at sea with the patrol only finishing on 22 January. Three days later *Puma* and *Salisbury* arrived at Farquhar and refuelled and Gan four days later. *Puma* finally arrived at Singapore on 4 February 1971.

After just three days alongside *Puma* and *Salisbury* slipped and made the journey to Hong Kong, where the pair arrived on 13 February 1971. Both ships received maintenance, whilst at the Colony. *Puma's* was completed on 8 March and upon leaving Hong Kong set course for Okinawa Exercise areas, where she stayed until 13 March. *Puma* was heading home to the United Kingdom, but had been given the so called 'Rich Man's Route' across the Pacific. March saw visits to Midway, Pearl Harbor, San Francisco and Monterey.

At Monterey a rodeo was laid on for the ships benefit and the *Puma's* team of would be cowboys succeeded in carrying off six of the champagne prizes for roping, hog-tying a steer and leaping on a piece of hide towed on the ground behind a horse at full gallop.

She entered the Panama Canal on 14 April and travelled through the waterway overnight, emerging into the Atlantic Ocean on the morning of the 15 April. *Puma* turned north and arrived at Chesapeake Bay on 20 April. There she operated with United States Navy vessels, which escorted the British frigate into the huge Norfolk Navy Base the next day. American hospitality lived up to reputation with barbeques and bars full of British servicemen and their American counterparts. *Puma* left Norfolk on 26 April and crossed the North Atlantic, arriving at Devonport's Number 5 wharf on 6 May 1971 after 174 days travelling around the world.

Maintenance was carried out on the frigate between 7 May and 10 June when she left for some weapons training until 25 June. The next morning *Puma* arrived at Troon, before exercising in the Clyde area until 4 July. The four-day passage to Gibraltar was followed by another spell of duty as Guardship at the Rock until 5 August.

During her time at Gibraltar *Puma's* team won the Top of the Rock race in a time of 25 minutes 16 seconds. Leading Steward Joe Cannon got to the top first and raised £42 for the ships Guide Dogs for the Blind fund. Following this success, *Puma* was to spend the next few weeks in the Mediterranean. For her last patrol there the planned schedule saw visits to Malta, Sete and La Maddalena before a return to Gibraltar on 24 August. Upon her arrival at Gibraltar *Puma* took over the role previously performed by sister ship *Leopard* of being command ship for the 10th Mine Counter Measures Squadron of the RNR during their annual *Mainhaul Exercise*. Admiral Commanding Reserves, Admiral I D McLaughton, CB, DSC joined *Puma* and flew his flag in the frigate.

At the end of the exercise *Puma* slipped away from the mine warfare vessels and arrived back at Devonport on 10 September. She was taken in hand for some maintenance, which lasted until 13 October. Two days later she arrived at Portsmouth for a ten-day stopover before more training at Portland throughout October and into November.

On 17 November she arrived at Devonport and dockyard workers alongside the ship's crew carried out essential maintenance on the ship and her systems. Towards the end of January 1972, *Puma* slipped from Devonport and sailed to Rosyth, where she arrived on 28 January. The frigate, with her long endurance diesel engines was an ideal vessel to dispatch on the fishery protection role off Iceland and Norway. She started her first fishery patrol on 31 January and would see her intercepting fishing vessels to check they were complying with all the stipulated rules. *Puma* remained on this duty in the North Sea until 26 February. Also in February it was announced that *Puma* would transfer homeport to Portsmouth in the future.

During her fishery patrol she visited Tromso, Hammerfest, Honningsvaag and a return visit to Tromso for two days starting on 21 February. Fishery Protection Patrol was an exhausting task for the crew of *Puma* and they were relieved by a two-day break at Greenock on 26 February. She remained in the area of the Clyde until 29 February, when she sailed to return to her new home port of Portsmouth. She sailed up the Solent on 2 March and secured at Portsmouth, where she remained until 15 March. She resumed her fishery protection duties with a visit to Oslo on St Patrick's Day and a port of call to Aberdeen a week later. After fuelling at Tromso on 1 April *Puma* arrived back at Portsmouth in time for Easter.

After Easter leave *Puma* left Portsmouth and headed for Portland on 15 May to continue crew training. By 22 May the frigate had arrived at Faslane, where she stayed until 6 June before sailing onto Campbeltown. *Puma* crossed the North Sea to visit Copenhagen on 10 June for a four-day visit to the Danish Capital. It was to be her last foreign visit before entering reserve. On 16 June she returned to Aberdeen, before sailing for Portsmouth, where she arrived on 23 June.

On 3 July 1972 *Puma* entered into a brief refit to prepare the ship to be reduced to care and maintenance. On 18 September 1972 she was towed from Portsmouth to Chatham to enter the Standby Squadron. The following year *Puma* was put on the disposal list. She remained in reserve for some years until she left Chatham under tow from the tug *RMAS Rollicker* arriving at C.F Booth Ltd in Blyth for breaking up on September 6 1976.

LINCOLN

The first steel for the construction of *Lincoln* was laid down on the slipway at Fairfield Shipbuilding and Engineering Co Ltd on 1 June 1955 and she was subsequently launched on 6 April 1959. The frigate's first commanding officer was Commander D W Napper MBE who joined the ship on 6 July 1960. The next day the warship was finally finished and in a ceremony was handed over to the Royal Navy.

As is normal practice, the next few months were spent bringing the ship up to full operational standard. These trials continued throughout the summer and into the autumn of 1960. On 20 October 1960 *Lincoln* left Milford Haven for Devonport to be taken in hand for engine repairs, which started on 24 October. The engine repairs were extensive and resulted in the ship remaining at Devonport Dockyard, throughout the winter of 1960 and well into 1961. Indeed, only on 24 February 1961 were the engine repairs finally completed.

More trials and evaluations continued throughout the spring of 1961 to prepare the frigate for her first Far East deployment. She remained in and around Devonport and the English Channel areas until *Lincoln* sailed to Gibraltar, where she arrived on 29 April. In May 1961 *Lincoln* teamed up with the aircraft carrier *Centaur* and the destroyer *Camperdown* and the US Navy Sixth Fleet for operations in the Mediterranean. After visiting Malta, where she worked up her Aircraft Direction equipment and skills, she called at Aden, Suez and Colombo on 29 May.

June saw the ship paying her first visits to Singapore, Hong Kong and Subic Bay on July 14. Four days later she sailed for a return visit to Singapore. When she left she assumed the role of Persian Gulf guardship, which lasted until 1 August when she put into Mombassa for a period of self-maintenance. After a fortnight in port, *Lincoln* sailed on 14 August to resume her Persian Gulf duties. There was another spell at Mombassa, before a visit to Bahrain on 9 September. En route to Singapore, *Lincoln* refuelled at Gan, and arrived at Singapore on 20 September.

Self-maintenance was carried out with minimal alongside assistance from the dockyard facilities, before she slipped from Singapore on 23 October for Hong Kong. The following months would see the frigate operating in support of British interests in the region with a full programme of exercises and port visits that kept the frigate fully occupied well into 1962.

On 1 February *Lincoln* arrived at Singapore before calling in at Calcutta on 10 February for a four-day visit. After a ten-day stop over at Singapore, *Lincoln* was detailed to take part in the annual *Exercise Jet* for eighteen days that also included two stops at Langkawi before the exercises finished on 17 March. A period of maintenance was followed by more exercises with Australian and American forces including *HMAS Melbourne* and *USS Yorktown*. *Exercise Sea Serpent* ended on 8 May and saw the huge fleet of no less than 57 SEATO ships at anchor in Manila Bay.

Indeed exercises were the order of 1962 with many undertaken throughout the frigate's time East of Suez. There were also port calls made to Hong Kong, Manila, Okinawa and Tawau. The highlight for many of the crew was the tour of Japanese port's, that started on 4 June when the frigate arrived at Yokosuka. *Lincoln* would also visit Nagoya and Beppu before arriving back at Singapore on 30 June.

On 12 July the frigate left for *FOTEX*, which continued until 27 July, after which she returned to Singapore. More exercises occupied *Lincoln*, before her arrival at Fremantle in Australia on 20 August for a four-day visit.

The small town of Bunbury was next on the agenda and *Lincoln* spent five days alongside at the town's port facilities before finally leaving on 30 August. On 15 September she arrived at Singapore for refit, which was completed on 29 December 1962.

New Year was celebrated alongside, but in January the ship was put through her paces during her post refit trials. February proved to be very busy indeed with her arrival at Langkawi for *Exercise Jet*. This annual exercise brought together warships from many Asian nations in order to improve working relationships in the region. The many and varied exercises continued throughout February and into March. When the ship arrived back at Singapore it was 18 March, but she only stayed overnight leaving soon after for Hong Kong with *Hermes*. After four days at sea the ships arrived at Hong Kong for a five-day stay. Back at Singapore and after some days alongside, *Lincoln* patrolled in the Tawau area in mid April, whilst the following month, she returned to Hong Kong. On 27 May *Lincoln* together with *Lion, Voyager* and *Hermes* left the colony and sailed for a tour of Japanese ports, calling at Osaka and Kobe before taking part in exercises in early June. Following the successful completion of these, *Lincoln* returned to patrolling the waters off Tawau, before arriving back at Singapore on 6 July.

On 25 July 1963 *Lincoln* left for exercises that would occupy her time until her return to Singapore on 9 August. Another exercise took he to sea again for a five-day period, three days later.

A third exercise took place between 16 and 21 September called *Exercise Dovetail* the exercise involved a number of Royal Navy units and some foreign participation. Four days later *Lincoln* sailed for Hong Kong, where she arrived on 28 September. Just over a week was spent alongside before sailing for Manila, where she would operate with the aircraft carrier *Victorious*. In November she visited Gan for an extended period, before returning to Singapore on 1 December. Christmas and New Year were celebrated at Singapore, but the New Year was barely one day old when on Thursday 2 January 1964 *Victorious* sailed from Singapore with *Diana, Lincoln* and the submarine *Andrew* to take part in a joint army support exercise called *'Cocktail'* off Malaya.

January would see the frigate operate off Tawau in support of Army units and visited Singapore before leaving at the end of the month to visit Hong Kong in early February. On Valentine's Day *Lincoln* was operating with the aircraft carrier *Centaur* during *Exercise Jet*, which continued until 17 February when the frigate arrived at Singapore, where *Lincoln* was taken in hand for a refit.

On 24 February 1964 Commander P F V Stigant assumed command and oversaw the final stages of her refit at Singapore. *Lincoln* commissioned on 7 March 1964. On 13 April *Lincoln* sailed with *Victorious, Parramatta, Yarra* and *Hampshire*.

The initial period of shakedown and work up was not-without incident. In the third week of the commission *Lincoln* was patrolling off Trenggannu looking for infiltrators, but without success. The patrol lasted for four days and the ship was recalled to Singapore for continuation of the work up.

The ship was officially declared operational on 1 May 1964 and sailed for Tawau. Having assumed the duties of guardship a good liaison was formed with the 1st/10th Gurhka's and 846 squadron. 'Lincoln's Inn' was established and a rest camp built on Sipiban Island. Men from the Ghurka's, 846 squadron and the ship were taken there and given two or three day banyan runs by a resident party from *Lincoln*.

From Tawau *Lincoln* sailed to Hong Kong. The stay was fraught with the Typhoon 'Winne' causing rough seas, although *Lincoln* passed some 350 miles away. *Lincoln* stayed in Hong Kong nearly three weeks and then returned to patrolling off Tawau. The Gurkha's changed with 42 Commando and Sipidan Island continued to flourish.

While patrolling off Tawau one afternoon a local fishing boat was seen weaving its way across the ocean, until it came to a gentle standstill on the edge of the islands reef. It was thought that rice wine had caused the accident. A small-scale salvage operation was mounted and the boat was towed off the reef, and into Tawau by *Lincoln*.

Lincoln returned to Singapore for post refit trials and work up which lasted until 21 January 1965. Spring 1965 was spent in the area off Tawau conducting anti-terrorism patrols off Indonesia and Malaya and in the course of these operations she intercepted numerous vessels. This policing mission was interspersed with both official and unofficial ports of call before returning to Singapore.

On 19 June *Lincoln* left Singapore and sailed for Hong Kong for a brief visit before retracing her passage back to Singapore. After a short maintenance period *Lincoln* took part in *Exercise Guardrail* between 16 and 26 August before returning to Singapore for a more extensive docking and maintenance period which was completed at the end of October. When she returned to sea in early November she operated with the aircraft carrier *Eagle* before visiting Tawau on 2 December. Four days later she pulled into the wide expanse of Hong Kong harbour for a ten-day stay. Christmas was to be celebrated at Singapore and accordingly the frigate slipped out of Hong Kong on 16 December to start the four-day passage back to Malaya.

During Christmas and New Year, the opportunity was taken to carry out some maintenance on the frigate, which lasted until 20 January 1966, when she started preparations for a major exercise in the area. *Exercise Mill-Stream* lasted for almost all of February and at its conclusion, *Lincoln* and the other participating vessels arrived at Singapore on 25 February.

Having sailed from Singapore in late February, *Lincoln* returned to Hong Kong on 1 March and remained there for the next twenty-day's undertaking some essential repairs to equipment onboard the frigate. She then sailed back to Singapore to start her journey back to the United Kingdom. On 11 April *Lincoln* waved Singapore goodbye and called at Gan for fuel and at Aden on 21 April. Three days later the frigate sailed north through the Suez Canal and entered into the Mediterranean. Two days were spent at Malta and another two days were spent at Gibraltar from 29 April. Finally, on 4 May 1966 after years away from home, *Lincoln* sailed past Devonport breakwater to enter into Devonport dockyard. Within weeks the frigate was taken in hand for a major refit.

Lincoln was at Devonport during Navy Days but was not open to the public. At this time the political fall out of the Rhodesian crisis caused one seaman on the frigate some misery. Midshipman Robert Fynn, aged 20 from Salisbury, Rhodesia was the only member of the ship's company without home leave. It was felt that the situation in the country was too dangerous to allow him home.

A much more pleasant visit was paid upon *Lincoln* when the Mayor and Mayoress of Plymouth were received onboard at a civic reception held onboard the frigate. After a buffet lunch in the wardroom with the officers the civic guests toured the ship and met six members of the Wrangler Sea Cadets Corps from the city of Lincoln who joined the ship from the destroyer *Hampshire* at Malta and sailed with *Lincoln* on the homeward voyage.

Throughout late 1967 preparations had been underway for an extensive refit on *Lincoln*. When she entered dry dock within Devonport Dockyard all her compartments were stripped out and refurbished. A new deckhouse was erected to house the SeaCat anti aircraft missile system and its associated directors and magazines. The mainmast was

167

plated over and modern electronic gear replaced obsolete equipment onboard. The refit was completed on 5 May 1968 and she was declared operational on 28 June.

In Early July *Lincoln* together with *Galatea, Diamond* and *Cavalier* exercised in the Western Approaches with the aircraft carrier *Hermes*. The force sailed to Gibraltar before returning to Devonport. *Lincoln* continued her work up's throughout late summer and autumn at Portland.

Lincoln sailed from the United Kingdom in November to go East of Suez under the command of Commander R J F Turner. She sailed south to South Africa. She would eventually spend one of the longest periods on the Beira patrol of any Royal Navy frigate.

Lincoln arrived at Singapore in March 1969. There the ship took part in the air/sea exercise *JULEX 69* for 18 days. British ships were the destroyer *London* and the assault ship *Fearless*, these ships were supported by a large frigate force of, *Danae, Cleopatra, Ajax, Juno, Argonaut,* and *Naiad*. There were also three submarines *Cachalot, Rorqual* and *Onslaught,* and RFA support came from *Resurgent, Tidereach, Tidesurge, Tidepool, Gold Rover* and the tug *Typhoon*. The exercise was under the command of Vice Admiral A T F G Griffin. The exercise began with a twelve-day weapons-training phase and was followed by a three-day tactical phase in which the fleet was subjected to air, submarine and fast attack craft attacks. All the Royal Navy ships returned to Singapore on July 24.

Lincoln went onto to visit Hong Kong, where sixteen members of the ship's crew built a slip way for children's boats on the island of Lan Tao, in a successful 'hearts and minds' operation. The slipway was built to get children's boats into the water without having to travel over rocks and glass for half a mile. Such roles were seen as important to building trust in the Royal Navy in foreign countries and these continued on visits to Japan and the Philippines. *Lincoln's* planned route home to the United Kingdom was to have seen her travelling via the so called 'rich mans' way home via Pearl Harbor, San Francisco, San Diego, Acapulco, Panama Canal and Bermuda. However, shortly before her departure from Singapore she was delayed by a defect and the visit to the United States had to be cancelled. On August 19 she sailed home via Gan and Simonstown, arriving back in the United Kingdom on October 3 and soon afterwards entered into a refit.

On 14 October Commander J G Brigham assumed command, but it would be sometime yet before he could take his new command to sea. *Lincoln* completed her docking period at Devonport on 20 January 1970. The remainder of January was spent conducting post refit trials at Portland before arriving back at Devonport on the last day of the month.

Lincoln left port on 2 February and headed for Gibraltar, where she took part in *GIBEX* until 17 February. The frigate was in the following two months scheduled to take part in the second phase of *GIBEX* and visit numerous ports of call including Malta before returning to Devonport on 21 March.

Easter leave was granted to the crew and when she left port again, her destination was once again the Mediterranean with a planned arrival at Gibraltar set for 6 April. There she assumed the role of guardship, before visiting Nice on 16 May for four-days. This was in turn followed by a short stop at Gibraltar preceding a return to Devonport.

On 6 July *Lincoln* sailed up the North Sea to Rosyth for exercises, which lasted until 16 July when the ship arrived at Leith. July also saw visits paid to Loch Ewe and Hull and time spent at sea operating with *Ark Royal*. A short stay at Portsmouth was followed by a return to Plymouth. She remained alongside the berth for the remainder of the month of August and was cleaned and polished to perfection for thousands of people during Navy Days.

Lincoln finally slipped from Devonport Dockyard on 7 September and arrived at Grimsby two days later. After five days spent in port, *Lincoln* slipped and headed across the North Sea and into the Baltic for what would become an historic visit designed to encourage trade between Britain and the Baltic states.

Lincoln together with the Tribal class frigate *Nubian* sailed on September 14 for the port of Lulea in Northern Sweden during the British Shopping Week. It was the first visit of a Royal Navy ship in living memory. Next port on the itinerary was the Finnish Capital Helsinki on September 23 for British Day during an international trade tour.

Receptions were planned for senior Finnish Government and trade officials onboard *Lincoln*, commanded by Commander J G Brigham and the *Nubian* with HRH Duke of Edinburgh as guest of honour. The two ships remained in Helsinki for the start of British Shopping Fortnight before sailing on September 28. Both events were part of a trade drive known as 'Britain in Finland 1970'.

Next port of call was the Swedish town of Galve for another British Shopping Week where the frigates arrived on 29 September. After this very successful, if unusual, visit, *Lincoln* sailed onto visit Wilshelmshaven in the beginning of October. On 14 October *Lincoln* sailed back into Devonport. Four days were spent alongside, before slipping and proceeding back to Chatham Dockyard, where preparations had been made to take her in hand for a refit.

Lincoln re-commissioned at Chatham on August 7 1971 and spent a week on post refit trials before returning to Chatham for Open Days on 29 and 30 August. Commander M H G Layard assumed command on the same day. The next month, whilst inside the dockyard the first recorded case of a life being saved in the dockyard by the use of the Kiss of Life took place onboard *Lincoln*. Lieutenant William Lampard used the technique on joiner John Hurt, who fell, sustaining head injuries whilst working on the frigate.

Lincoln left Chatham Dockyard on 13 September and anchored off Margate for three days before returning to Chatham. Further equipment and crew trials continued throughout the remainder of September, until *Lincoln* was declared operational on 18 October. Even more trials and evaluations were carried out off Portland until she arrived at Portsmouth on 6 November. Almost a week later *Lincoln* was back at Chatham Dockyard to undertake repairs to a defective crankshaft, which meant the frigate remained in port throughout the winter months.

In January 1972 *Lincoln* was at Chatham Dockyard and engine fitters, shipwrights and slinger's who replaced the defective crankshaft in one of *Lincoln's* engines claimed a new record for the task. The job was scheduled to take eight men working twelve-hour shifts six days. The task actually took seven men working only eight-hour shifts and five days to complete. When *Lincoln* left Chatham she carried out more trials off Portland until 24 February. After spending four days at Devonport, *Lincoln* visited HMS Ganges on 1 March during a visit to Harwich. The next day she arrived at Rosyth to take part in *JMC 164* until 23 March. Four days were spent at Grimsby until 28 March, before starting a maintenance period at Chatham Dockyard on 29 March where she remained until 12 May.

After a few days at Portsmouth, she left on 15 May to undertake the passage to Portland, to prepare for her major deployment to the Far East. *Lincoln* paid port visits to Gibraltar, Las Palmas and Ascension Island before arriving at Simonstown on 7 June. The usual round of social and sporting activities usually against the South African Navy took place. Many of the ships' company also took the opportunity to undertake some individual pursuits such as rock climbing. Eight days later *Lincoln* slipped from the Naval base and headed for Reunion Island, which was reached on 21 June.

In July *Lincoln* had reached the Philippines and was in Subic Bay when she received an urgent request for assistance from the Indonesian government after a fortnight of some of the heaviest rainfall ever recorded in the region. The area was severely flooded and in some areas up to 150 inches of rain had fallen in just fourteen days, especially on the island of Zomboanga. There the residents were desperate for food and other supplies. The frigate quickly loaded 'a vast amount of tinned milk and various medical stores before sailing'. Having left Subic *Lincoln* arrived off Lingauen, where the supplies were offloaded by boat by 30 ratings working in a chain.

On 21 August 1972 Commander John D H B Howard assumed command for what proved to be a very busy deployment. *Lincoln* arrived at the Indonesian Capital of Djakarta on September 29 from Zomboanga in the Philippines where the previous weekend, the ship was awarded the presidential citation for her relief works in the republic.

After a maintenance period at Singapore, *Lincoln* prepared to commence the journey home to the United Kingdom. By 5 January 1973 she had arrived at Gibraltar. After a few days spent at the Rock, *Lincoln* arrived on 18 January. Five days later she was back home at Chatham Dockyard, where she was docked down until 2 March. The next day *Lincoln* returned to sea to start her trials.

Further trials were conducted in and around Portsmouth and Portland, before taking part in *JMC 167* until 4 April at Rosyth. Two days later *Lincoln* had sailed up the River Medway and secured within Chatham Dockyard. Easter leave was granted and upon the crew's return, *Lincoln* slipped and set a course for the Western Isles of Scotland. She would go onto visit a number of small ports in the region, including Oban, Tobermory, Kyle of Lochalsh and Portree. Having left the beautiful isles behind, *Lincoln* paid a four-day official visit to the city of Liverpool on 4 May. This was followed by a period of time spent at Portland, before sailing onto Portsmouth for a maintenance period, which was completed on 18 June.

On 22 June *Lincoln* crossed the English Channel and visited the French port of Le Harve for a couple of days, before going on to Kolding. Then Rosyth was visited to stock up on supplies before sailing north to Iceland to participate in a fishery patrol off Iceland, which started on 4 July.

This operation produced heated debate between the two nations and accordingly in order to protect British trawlers the Royal Navy sent numerous frigates to the area to undertake this task. The Fishery Patrol usually involved boarding trawlers to check they complied with all the regulations, but when Icelandic gunboats threatened British trawlers, *Lincoln* was there to protect them.

On one occasion the trawler support vessel *Othello* presented the frigate with a 200-pound Halibut, a giant specimen. Three cooks on *Lincoln* cut the Halibut into steaks for the ships' company supper. So much fish was onboard that the frigate's crew ate 650 pounds worth of fish in just four weeks. The Icelandic gunboats became increasingly aggressive and on 17 July 1973 *Lincoln* was slightly damaged by collision with the Icelandic *Aegir* off Iceland's South East Coast. *Lincoln's* captain, Commander Howard acted swiftly during the encounters with the Icelandic gunboats, on numerous occasions it was only by skill that both ships were not severely damaged. During a particular patrol there occurred a certain incident, now known as the 'Bottle of Whiskey' incident. The

Icelandic gunboat manoeuvred so close to the British frigate that at times the two ships were only 15 inches apart. Commander Howard held up a bottle of whiskey to the Icelandic ship in a gesture designed to calm the situation. The Icelandic captain it was felt quite rudely pulled his ship away sharply.

On 30 July *Lincoln* returned to Chatham Dockyard and following repairs was opened to the public at Chatham Navy Days over the weekend of Sunday and Monday 26 and 27 August. The Fishery Patrol role resumed when *Lincoln* left Chatham Dockyard and headed back to the Cold Icelandic waters and to the Cod War.

The collisions continued and upon her return to Chatham Dockyard on Thursday 27 September, *Lincoln* was inspected and surveyed by dockyard workers after suffering a number of collisions in the Icelandic waters. After being accessed as satisfactory, the frigate entered into a period of routine maintenance within the dockyard.

On 2 November Commander Howard visited Medway Hospital in Chatham and took a luxury cake to the children's ward at the hospital. Upon his return to his ship, *Lincoln* sailed for *JMC 169* until mid November. After visiting Rosyth and Leith, *Lincoln* took part in *Exercise Ocean Span* until 30 November. There was a short port of call at Hull, before the frigate returned home to Chatham Dockyard on 5 December.

After seasonal leave had been taken the crew returned to the ship and after leaving Chatham in early January 1974 set sail for Portsmouth, for a period of Navigational Training. On 28 January *Lincoln* left Portsmouth Dockyard for Weapons training that took the ship through to the beginning of February. Upon her return to Portsmouth, the frigate was docked for four days until 8 February. Three days later she slipped and headed south for Gibraltar for duties as guardship.

After her duties at Gibraltar were completed on 11 March, she sailed north to Penzance for a few days. She then crossed the North Sea and visited Kolding for a five-day visit before returning to Portsmouth on 29 March.

On 3 April *Lincoln* arrived at Devonport and started her refit on 15 April. Three days later saw the appointment of Lieutenant Commander J Page as her commanding officer during the refit. Once the brief refit was completed, she was paid off and placed into the reserve fleet at Chatham.

The pressure of having enough frigates to patrol the increasingly hostile waters around Iceland during the Cod War and the damage inflicted upon active ships in the fleet meant that those ships in the standby squadron were re-activated, albeit briefly. *Lincoln* was one of these ships and on 27 May 1976 Commander I Lachlan assumed command of the frigate. Most of her last commission was spent on Icelandic fishery patrol duties. In late summer the frigate returned to her homeport and *Lincoln* was at Navy Days, but not open to the public.

Lincoln's final refit was carried out at Devonport, and after its completion the ship paid a visit to Grimsby as it is the closest port to the city of Lincoln Grimsby. It was soon apparent that Lincoln and Grimsby were competing for the title of best hosts, eventually Lincoln won in a good-hearted competition.

The *Lincoln* put up a football team to take on a team of female police officers from Lincoln constabulary. The men were dressed in female costumes of sorts, but the girls got the men handcuffed and sent off.

This was, however, the twilight of the frigate's career and after a brief refit at Devonport she sailed on November 29 flying her paying off pennant as she passed the Narrows and steered around Drakes Island. Onboard for the final journey was the Mayor of Lincoln, Mr Cecil Robinson, The Sheriff Mr E J Thimblerby and the Mayor's officers. As she sailed out she was met by gale force storm but was saluted for the last time by Vice Admiral Gordon Tait, Flag Officer Plymouth who was on the saluting base at Admiralty House.

Once at Chatham *Lincoln* paid off into reserve at Chatham Dockyard. She was mothballed in the Standby Squadron and many people did not expect the frigate to return to service with the Royal Navy. She was, however, maintained to a high standard in case she was needed. Two years later an arms deal was struck between the British and Egyptian governments, *Lincoln, Salisbury* and the County class destroyer *Devonshire* were sold to the Egyptian navy. A large amount of work was undertaken to restore the frigate to operational condition prior to handing over, but at the last moment the Egyptian's cancelled the deal and *Lincoln* was returned to reserve at Chatham.

In July 1979 *Lincoln* was at Chatham Dockyard and was being re-equipped on an opportunity basis in preparation for reserve with the Standby Squadron. The following month the decision was taken to use the frigate as a 'Submarine Practice Ship'. She was taken to the Clyde areas and used for some months in this role.

Following this period in her career, *Lincoln*, once more returned to Chatham Dockyard and the Standby Squadron where she became the last ship to be laid up at Chatham Dockyard. She remained there for the next few months, until John Nott's infamous 1981 Defence Review. *Lincoln*, along with many of her sister ships and those of the Leopard class were declared surplus to requirements and were quickly sold for scrap. For *Lincoln*, the future, for a time looked promising as Bangladeshi officials discussed the possibility of buying the frigate as a running mate to *Umar Farooq* (ex *Llandaff*). Unfortunately a deal was not struck and *Lincoln* continued to languish at Chatham Dockyard. It would, however, be almost another two years before she was sold for scrapping. On 20 April 1983 *Lincoln* was towed from Chatham Dockyard to Inverkeithing to be broken up. After four days at sea she arrived at the ship breaker's under the tow of local tugs *Gurnet* and *Inchcolm*.

BRAHMAPUTRA

(Ex PANTHER)

Originally the Leopard class was to total five units in Royal Navy service and accordingly a contract was placed for a fifth frigate with John Brown's shipyard at Glasgow. On 20 October 1955 *Panther* was laid down. Construction progressed well, but later when India expressed an interest in buying British designed warships, the *Panther* was released, to the Indian Navy, and construction continued as the *Brahmaputra*.

She was launched on 15 March 1957 and completed on 31 March 1958 and was formally commissioned into Royal Indian Navy service. Initially the ship carried out her builder's trials in and around the Clyde and around the Isle of Arran. Upon her acceptance by Indian Navy representatives at the shipyard, *Brahmaputra* continued her trials at Portland, English Channel and Western Approaches.

In late summer 1958 the frigate sailed to India with the usual stopovers at Gibraltar, Malta and Port Said before transiting the Suez Canal en route to her operating base of Bombay.

Brahmaputra, along with her sister-ships *Betwa* and *Beas* operated throughout the frequent border disputes and full-blown wars between India and Pakistan throughout the 1960's and 1970's. *Brahmaputra*, herself, took part in numerous actions where her twin 4.5" turrets and accurate fire proved invaluable in naval bombardments.

In 1978 *Brahmaputra* was taken in hand for a refit that saw the aft 4.5" gun removed and replaced with classrooms for training purposes. As such the frigate served in a training capacity along with *Beas* and *Betwa* in the 16th Frigate Squadron.

The frigate remained virtually unaltered throughout the remainder of her career in the Indian Navy that finally came to an end when *Brahmaputra* was deleted in 1986 and quickly was sold for scrap.

BEAS

Beas was ordered in 1954 from Vickers on the Tyne. She was laid down on 29 November 1956. *Beas* was launched on October 9 1958. The naming was performed by Mrs R S David wife of Captain R S David, naval adviser to the High Commissioner for India in the United Kingdom. 3 April 1960 the ship had a new commanding officer in the shape of Commander B R Kapoor. On 24 May 1960 the frigate was finally completed and handed over to the Indian Navy.

After builder's trials the ship entered Portsmouth Dockyard and then later worked up in and around Portland, sometimes with her British sister ships. After these trials were completed the *Beas* started her journey to her new home with visits to Gibraltar, Malta and the Suez Canal before crossing the Indian Ocean and arriving at Bombay, which would become her home for the best part of her career with the Indian Navy.

On 9 October 1961 Commander T J Kunnerkeril joined the ship and replaced Commander B R Kapoor in command of the frigate. Commander Kunnerkeril, would barely two months later take the *Beas* to war over Goa. By 1 December 1961, the Indian Naval Headquarters had instituted a surveillance exercise called *Operation Chutney*. On the first day of the operation, two frigates, *INS Betwa* and *INS Beas*, started patrolling off the Goa coastline at a distance of 13 kilometres. They reported on all shipping movements and were under orders to retaliate if engaged by Portuguese units. The only Portuguese ship in port was the frigate, *Alfonso de Albuquerque*.

The Indian plan called for the capture of Goa, Mormugao Bay and Aguada, Daman, Diu and Anjadiv island. Another group of warships would destroy the coastal batteries and attack Portuguese warships. To accomplish these tasks the Indian Navy task force was divided into four distinct groups. The surface action group comprised the cruiser *INS Mysore*, the destroyer *INS Trishul,* and frigates *INS Betwa, INS Beas* and *INS Cauvery*. The Carrier Task Group was centred on the Indian Navy's sole aircraft carrier

INS Vikrant, with her escort that comprised *INS Delhi, INS Kuthar, INS Kirpan, INS Khukri* and *INS Rajput.* The third group was a minesweeping group and the fourth group was the Support Group with just *INS Dharini* allocated to it.

After almost two weeks of waiting on 18-19 December 1961, the Government of India adopted a plan called *Operation Vijay* to liberate the Portuguese colonies in India. By 11 December 1961, Indian forces were placed at Belgaum, Vapi and Una, for attacks on Goa, Daman and Diu, respectively. The Portuguese deployed four frigates the *Alfonso de Albuquerque, Bartholomeu Dias, Gonsalves Zarco* and *Joao de Lisboa.* During the action that followed, however, three of the ships had already left leaving just the *Alfonso de Albuquerque* to defend Goa.

The tension mounted in the area, when the Portuguese fired on and hit the Indian steam ship *Sabarmati,* killing an Indian fisherman and injuring the ships' chief engineer.

Operation Vijay was a success and the capture of Anjadiv Island was completed on 18 December 1961.

The ship took part in many of the conflicts with Pakistan, especially throughout the 1970's and fired many times on enemy vessels during these brief but bloody wars. In 1972 *Beas* was severely damaged when the cruiser *Mysore* collided with the frigate. *Beas* was subsequently repaired and returned to service. Towards the end of *Beas* career she, like her sisters was relegated to the secondary role of training and as such had a new deckhouses built aft, which replaced the after 4.5" gun and served as training ships as part of the 16th frigate squadron. *Beas* was modernised in 1980 and amongst other improvements her 40mm GFCS radar being removed.

The Indian Navy finally deleted *Beas* from the fleet in 1988 and it was not long before she was sold for scrap and demolition work was underway within a year on the frigate.

BETWA

Betwa was laid down at Vickers Armstrong yard on the Tyne on 29 May 1957. Her construction was relatively uncomplicated and in a ceremony attended by officials from the Indian navy and Indian embassy in London, she was launched into the waters of the River Tyne on 15 May 1959. Fitting out and trials continued until she was finally completed on 8 December 1960.

After builder's trials in the North Sea, the Indian Navy took advantage of the extensive facilities around Portland to trial the ship further before finally sailing for India.

During the liberation of Goa by Indian forces, the Portuguese frigate *Alfonso de Albuquerque* was at anchorage at Momugao Bay on 18 December 1961. *INS Betwa* was ordered to capture the vessel and she commenced on closing in on the warship. At 12.15 hours, INS *Betwa* commenced firing with her 4.5" guns and shortly *Albuquerque* surrendered and beached herself off Dona Paula jetty. Following the sinking of *Albuquerque*, the Indian Navy continued patrolling till 19 December 1961 and thereafter ships were ordered to return back to Bombay. All operations in Goa came to an end at 6pm on 19 December 1961.

All three Indian ships had new deckhouses built aft which replaced the after 4.5" gun and all served as training ships as part of the 16th Frigate Squadron. In 1988 *Betwa* formed part of the training squadron at Cochin and was replaced soon after and all too soon the ship was sold for scrap.

COMMANDING OFFICERS

JAGUAR

Cdr Bellingham

Cdr M C Clapp

Cdr D T Goodhugh

Cdr P W Greening

Lt Cdr M G Moberly

Cdr D I Rhodes

Cdr J B Robatham

Cdr L M N Saunders

LINCOLN

Cdr J G Brigham

Cdr J D H B Howard

Cdr M H G Layard

Cdr J Page

Cdr D W Napper

Cdr P F V Stigant

SALISBURY

Cdr H M Ellis

Cdr W Fitzgerald

Cdr I F Grant

Cdr R D Johnson

Lt Cdr J T Sanders

Cdr J K Stevens

Cdr A G Watson

Cdr H M White

Cdr F N Ponsonby

LLANDAFF

Cdr I F O Alford

Cdr I R Bowden

Cdr I M V Browne

Lt Cdr William

Cdr J S Kelly

Cdr I B Lennox

Cdr Colin Marr

Cdr George Oxley

Corry Cdr R A Snow

Cdr Stephen Alexander Stuart

PUMA

Cdr R P Clayton

Capt C J Cunningham

Cdr N A D Grant

Lt Cdr P Harries

Cdr J Marriott

Cdr D B N Mellis DSC

Cdr A M G Pearson

Cdr J F H C de Winton

Capt M N Lucey DSC

CHICHESTER

Lt Cdr Butt

Cdr D W Foster

Cdr T D Kitson

Cdr E H M Orme

Cdr G A Rowan-Thomson

Lt Cdr T J Sex

Cdr R P Warwick

Cdr N H N Wright

Lt Cdr Ranger

LEOPARD

Cdr J A D Ford

Lt Cdr D C Griffiths

Cdr P S Hicks-Beach

Cdr M J A Hornblower

Cdr A D Hutton

Cdr N R D King

Lt Cdr C A Nix

Cdr R H Whyte-Melville Jackson

LYNX

Lt Cdr A J N Allenby

Capt P M Austin

Lt Cdr G A Cole

Capt J M D Gray OBE

Capt J G Jungius

Cdr C H Layman

Capt W G Meeke MBE DSC

Capt P G R Mitchell

Lt Cdr N St.J Morley Hall

Cdr B Prideaux

Cdr G J F Slocock

Cdr A J White

CONSTRUCTION

NAME	PENNANT	BUILDER	LAID DOWN	LAUNCHED	COMPLETED
Salisbury	F32	HM Devonport	23/1/52	25/6/53	27/2/57
Leopard	F14	HM Portsmouth	25/3/53	23/5/55	30/9/58
Chichester	F59	Fairfield Shipbuilding	26/6/53	21/4/55	16/5/58
Lynx	F27	J Brown & Co Ltd	15/8/53	12/1/55	14/3/57
Llandaff	F61	Hawthorn Leslie	27/8/53	30/11/55	11/4/58
Jaguar	F37	W. Denny & Bros	2/11/53	20/7/57	12/12/59
Puma	F34	Scotts Shipbuilding	16/11/53	30/6/54	27/4/57
Lincoln	F99	Fairfield Shipbuilding	1/6/55	6/4/59	7/7/60
Panther/					
(Brahmaputra)	F31	J Brown & Co Ltd	20/11/55	15/3/57	31/3/58
Beas	F37	Vickers Tyne	29/11/56	9/10/58	24/5/60
Betwa	F38	Vickers Tyne	29/5/57	15/9/59	8/12/60

SPECIFICATIONS

Leopard class Type 41 frigates

Displacement: 2,300 tons standard; 2,520 tons full load

Length: 340ft

Beam: 40ft

Draught: 16ft

Armament: 4 x 4.5" DP guns in two Mk IV turrets. 2 x40mm anti aircraft guns on Mk V mountings. 1 x Squid ASW launcher.

Sonars: Type 170, 174.

Machinery: 8 x Admiralty Standard Range ASR1 diesels driving two shafts.

Speed: 24 knots

Oil fuel: 220 tons

Complement: 205 (later rising to 235)

Salisbury class Type 61 frigates

Displacement: 2,170 tons standard, 2,400 tons full load

Length: 340ft overall

Beam: 40ft

Draught: 15.5ft

Armament: 2 x 4.5" DP in one Mk IV turret forward. 2 x 40mm AA guns on a STAAG mounting. (1 x 40mm gun on Lincoln). 1 x Squid ASW launcher. Later Salisbury, Lincoln later received the SeaCat anti aircraft missile system during refits.

Sonars: Types 170, 174.

Machinery: 8 x Admiralty Standard Range (ASR1) diesels driving two shafts.

Speed: 24 knots

Oil fuel: 230 tons

Complement: 207 (later rising to 237)

184

PREVIOUS SHIPS OF THE NAME

JAGUAR

The first *Jaguar* was a destroyer of the Javelin class, was laid down at Denny Bros, yard in Dumbarton on 25 November 1937. She was launched on 22 November 1938 and completed on 12 September 1939. Following builder's trials the new destroyer was attached to the 7th Destroyer Flotilla in the Humber Force at Grimsby on 26 September. She was attacked twice by bombers but survived with no damage. *Jaguar* was then given the duty of anti submarine patrols and escort duties off the East Coast until the end of 1940.

Jaguar was one of the ships that operated as part of *Operation Quixote*, which successfully cut six telegraph-cables between the East Coast of England and Borkum and Nordeney to prevent their use by the enemy. She played an active role in *Operation Dynamo* and took many soldiers from the beaches of Dunkirk. Unfortunately, Jaguar was struck by bombs from German dive-bombers and was towed back to Dover, where she was repaired

Further operations included *Operation Medium* on 11 October 1940 when she shelled Cherbourg, with the battleship *Revenge* and destroyers of the 5th Flotilla. On 27 November 1940 *Jaguar* took part in the famous action off Cape Spartivento.

1941 saw the destroyer in the heat of the action in the Mediterranean that included *Operation Ration*, the interception of Vichy ships and an engagement with the Italian destroyer *Crispi* on the night of 27/28 February 1941. This took place as *Jaguar* covered the landing of troops at Castelorizo. Later in May *Jaguar* took part in the battle for Crete whilst June saw her operating with Force H. *Jaguar* took part in July's campaign. The war in the Mediterranean was frantic and saw a great deal of losses on both sides. On 20 December she rescued 8 officers and 17 ratings from the destroyer *Kandahar* which had struck a mine off Tripoli. *Jaguar* sank the crippled destroyer.

On 26th March 1942, while escorting the RFA tanker *Slavol, Jaguar* was sunk by U652 (Kapitaneutnant Georg-Werner Fraatz) in position 31'53N-26'18E, north of Sollum/Sidi Barrani. One hundred and ninety three men lost their lives, but eight-officers and forty-five ratings were rescued by the anti submarine whaler *Klo*. The same U-boat later also sank the *Slavol*.

Battle honours for the name *Jaguar*

Dunkirk 1940, Atlantic 1940, Spartivento 1940, Matapan 1941, Crete 1941, Mediterranean 1941, Libya 1941-42, Malta Convoys 1941-1942.

LEOPARD

There have been twelve previous ships bearing the name *Leopard* that have served in the Royal Navy. The first was a ship with an armament of 34 guns. She was built in 1635 and surrendered to the enemy in 1652.

The second ship called *Leopard* was by 1659 hulked and eventually sunk as a foundation in 1699, but not before gaining a number of battle honours, notably the battle of Lowestoft in 1665, Four Day's Battle in 1666, Orfordness 1666, Solebay 1672 and Texel in 1673.

The next *Leopard* was a 4th rate built in 1703 and like her immediate predecessor added to the battle honours. She participated fully in the battles at Marbella in 1705 and Gaspe in 1711. After a long and worthy career, *Leopard* was broken up in 1740. The following year her replacement, another 4th rate was constructed. After twenty years of service she was broken up.

The sixth *Leopard* was yet again another 4th rate and was built in 1782.

The seventh *Leopard* another 4th rate took part in the famous battle off Egypt in 1801. However, in 1814 during a bad storm the ship was wrecked with much loss of life.

The name of *Leopard* slipped out of usage until 1850 when a frigate with the name was constructed. This warship would garner the last three of *Leopard's* battle honours, those of Baltic 1854, Black Sea 1855 and Simonseki 1864. *Leopard* was sold out of Royal Navy service in 1867.

The eleventh *Leopard* was a destroyer and commissioned into service in 1897. She served throughout the First World War and was finally decommissioned and sold in 1919. An ex French destroyer was used by the Royal Navy briefly in 1940 and was renamed *Leopard.*

In 1955 *Leopard* became the lead ship in a class of four anti aircraft frigates.

Battle Honours for the name LEOPARD

Lowestoft 1665, Four Day's Battle 1666, Orfordness 1666, Solebay 1672, Texel 1673, Marbella 1705, Gaspe 1711, Egypt 1801, Baltic 1854, Black Sea 1855, Simonseki 1864.

PANTHER

The first *Panther* was a 4th rate built in 1703. She was present at the battle of Velez Malaga the following year and gave the name her first battle honour. The ship was subsequently hulked and sold out of service in 1768 after having been renamed. Previously in 1746 the name *Panther* was given to a new 4th rate vessel, which served well until 1756 when she was broken up. Two years later another 4th rate was commissioned that served until 1813. It would be another eighty-three years before the name *Panther* reappeared when it was given to a destroyer that commissioned in 1896. This destroyer served throughout the First World War and was finally sold out of service in 1920.

Another twenty-one years would elapse before the name was again given to a destroyer. In this case a P class destroyer built on 28 May 1941. *Panther* was escorting the cruiser *Carlisle* and was struck by concentrated air attack by German Stuka's and was sunk off Scarpanto Straits in position 35.48'N, 27.38'E.

LYNX

The first *Lynx* appeared in 1761 when a sloop was commissioned. Sixteen years later she passed out of service and was replaced the same year with a new *Lynx*. This ship would only serve for six years before being sold.

The next ship to bear the name *Lynx* was another sloop, commissioned into service in 1794. *Lynx* served the Royal Navy until 1813

The sixth *Lynx* was a 160hp-screw vessel of four guns that took part in the bombardment of Sebastapol during the Crimean War. The same ship also took part in an expedition to the Sea of Azov and in Livingstone's expedition into Africa.

The last ship to carry the name *Lynx* was a 21-knot torpedo boat destroyer of the 4th TBD Flotilla in the Grand Fleet.

Lynx was a WW1 British destroyer serving with the 4th destroyer Flotilla of the Grand Fleet based at Scapa Flow. She had been built by London and Glasgow Shipbuilding of Glasgow in 1913 and was lost when she struck a mine in the Moray Firth on 9 August 1915. Her captain, Cdr J F H Cole RN was one of the 70 men who lost their lives. Out of a crew of 96 only 4 officers and 22 men survived the blast. Her remains were rediscovered on 7 August 2000 by a diving team from Wick in Scotland

In 1939 the Royal Navy base at Dover took over the name *Lynx*, but with the end of the war, the need to maintain a permanent presence at the Kent port was not necessary and the base was closed in 1946.

PUMA

Surprisingly the frigate of 1955 was the first Royal Navy warship to use the name.

SALISBURY

There have been six warships named after the city. The first was a 4th rate with 48 guns. She had a displacement of 682 bm and was built at Bucklers Hard in Hampshire in 1698. Five years later the French captured her on 10 April 1703, but was recaptured fter five years serving the enemy on 15 March 1708. On 2 January 1716 she was renamed *Preston* and continued to serve for another twenty-six years until she was rebuilt in 1742. Six years later whilst at Trincomalee she was sold and broken up the following year.

The second *Salisbury* was another 4th rate of 703bm and was constructed at Chatham Dockyard and launched on 3 July 1707. Later she was rebuilt at Portsmouth Dockyard in 1726. By 1744 she was a hulk and sold out of service five years later.

Another 4th rate followed in 1745. This vessel was built by Ewer at East Cowes and was condemned on 24 April 1761 whilst in the East Indies.

Yet another 4th rate with 50 cannons followed with its launch on 2 October 1769 at Chatham Dockyard. This *Salisbury* displaced 1,051bm. After a very successful career lasting almost thirty years, *Salisbury* was wrecked on 13 May 1796 on rocks near San Domingo.

The final 4th rate to bear the name *Salisbury* was built at Deptford Dockyard and was launched on 21 June 1814. She was armed with 58 cannons on three decks and displaced 1,199 bm. Her service life was comparative short and she was sold out of service in 1837 to Beatson for breaking up.

During the Second World War, the sixth warship to bear the name *Salisbury* was one of fifty US destroyers delivered to the United Kingdom under the terms of the lend/lease agreement. *Salisbury* was formerly **USS Claxton** of 1,090 tons. Armed with one 4-inch gun and 1 3-inch gun. These were backed up with four 20mm and three torpedo tubes. *Salisbury* commissioned into service on 5 December 1940. With the turn in fortunes in the Battle of the Atlantic the ship was subsequently lent to the Royal Canadian Navy between September 1942 and 1944. *Salisbury* was sold on 26 June 1944 in Canada.

LLANDAFF

There has only been the one ship to bear this name in the Royal Navy and that is the Type 61 frigate.

LINCOLN

There have been three ships called *Lincoln* with the first being a 4th rate with 48 guns. She was constructed at Woolwich and launched on 19 February 1695. After only eight years of service the ship foundered in a storm on 29 January 1703 with substantial loss of life.

The second ship to be christened *HMS Lincoln* was another lend/lease US destroyer. The former *USS Yarnall* of 1,090 tons was transferred to the Royal Navy and commissioned in October 1940. The following September the ship was lent to the Royal Norwegian Navy and after three years was then transferred to the Russian Navy, who renamed the ship *Druzni* on 26 August 1944. She served in the Arctic and elsewhere until 19 August 1952 when she was finally sailed back to the United States. In September 1952 she was sold at Charleston.

CHICHESTER

There have been six Royal Navy warships to bear the name *Chichester*, with the first, a 2nd rate, entering service in 1695 having been built at Chatham Dockyard. Eleven years later the ship was entirely rebuilt at Woolwich Dockyard. The ship continued, in service for another forty-three years, before being broken up at Plymouth at the end of 1749.

A 3rd rate ship followed and was built at Portsmouth Dockyard and was completed on 4 June 1753. Fifty years later she was broken up.

Chichester was the name chosen in 1785 for a 5th rate with forty-four guns and 901bm. The ship was built by the yard of Taylor at Itchenor and was handed over to the Royal Navy on 10 March 1785. By 1799 she had been reduced to a store ship and was soon thereafter lent to the West India Dockyard Company to act as a training ship. In June 1815 she was scrapped.

The fourth ship to bear the name *Chichester* also had one of the most dramatic careers. Commissioned as Storeship 26 of just 777 bm, she would later be captured by the French warship *Belle Poule* off Valona and was renamed *Var* on 15 February 1809. In French hands the ship did not fare well and was wrecked off Madras on 2 May 1811.

The fifth ship was a 4th rate with fifty-two cannons and was built at Woolwich Dockyard and was completed on 12 July 1843. Her early career was not particularly spectacular as the ship was almost immediately laid up at Chatham until sold as a training ship in 1866. She was sold to Castle for breaking up in May 1889.

INDEX

193

195

197

198

199

Ushuaia, 31